Tschüs

HUGO'S SIM

GERMAN
IN THREE MONTHS

American
10:30 = halb elf Germ

HUGO'S LANGUAGE BOOKS LTD
LONDON

**Revised and rewritten by
Ann Friedlaender**

ISBN 0 85285 054 9

This Edition 1987

PRINTED AND BOUND IN GREAT BRITAIN BY
HAZELL WATSON AND VINEY LTD
AYLESBURY, BUCKS

Preface

In preparing Part I of this Grammar, we have assumed that the reader wants to learn German from a practical angle and have accordingly set out those rules that will be of most use to him or her in this respect. The order in which they are given also takes the need for rapid progress into consideration. This order is combined with exercises containing sentences of as practical a nature as is possible within the limitations of the concurrent vocabulary, so that you will be able to put your knowledge of the language to use at an early stage. The verbs have been simplified as much as possible; for detailed reference (complete conjugation tables and so forth) we recommend our *German Verbs Simplified*. The Hugo system of Imitated Pronunciation makes everything so much easier for the absolute beginner, as do our cassette and disc recordings of this book.

In Part II we progress to the use of idiom and common colloquial expressions, and then to reading practice. Any serious student of the language will need to have a thorough grasp of such things, and the less dedicated will find that the business of language learning takes on a new (and much brighter) light when the living idiomatic language is displayed. With an eye to the needs of the visitor to Germany, we have included specialized vocabularies on such subjects as travel, clothing, shops, food, and so on. These lists do not merely constitute a sort of phrase book; use them together with the words and constructions already learnt in Part I, interchange them and thus consolidate your knowledge of the language.

Part III consists of the answers to the grammar exercises in Part I. Advice on how to tackle these exercises will be found in the Introduction to Part I on p. 7.

Contents

PART I

Introduction	7
Pronunciation	9
Explanation of Grammatical Terms	13
Lessons One to Twenty-Four	15–135
Grammar, Exercises and Conversational Sentences	

PART II

Introduction	139
Idioms	140
Reading Texts	146
Hesse, Borchert, Böll	
Vocabularies	158
Travelling, Shops and Services, Clothing,	
Parts of the Body, Eating and Drinking	

PART III

Key to Grammar Exercises in Part I	177
Index	190

GERMAN
IN THREE MONTHS

I

GRAMMAR SIMPLIFIED
EXERCISES AND VOCABULARIES
CONVERSATION

Introduction

The following pages contain rules on pronunciation with which you are advised to make yourself familiar before starting the first lesson, (preferably with the aid of the recorded material). There is no need to learn these rules by heart at this stage; by referring back to them at frequent intervals you will soon know them well. For a while the Imitated Pronunciation of each new word is given as it is introduced into your vocabulary (see end of Lesson Seven).

There is also an explanation of some of the grammatical terms used in the book, which may serve as reference.

In studying the lessons, first read each rule carefully, comparing with the examples underneath. Then translate the exercise which follows, checking against the key at the back. Sentences to be translated from German to English are only given in the early lessons. The conversational sentences should be read aloud and their construction carefully noted. If you have the records or cassette tapes, listen to them first when reading the examples, the exercise answers and conversational sentences. Try to understand as you listen and then imitate what you hear as closely as possible.

As you progress, try to make up your own sentences based on the examples given and using the vocabulary you have learnt.

Pronunciation

The German language is pronounced as it is written, so once the pronunciation of the letters is learnt, it is quite easy to say every word. Most words have the stress on the first syllable unless they begin with one of the unaccented prefixes: **be-, ge-, er-, ver-, zer-, emp-, ent-.** Such prefixes and also endsyllables are sounded only very slightly. In our Imitated Pronunciation the stressed syllable is shown with an accent mark after it; thus the word **Esel** is imitated as ay'-sel, showing stress on the first syllable.

Vowels are generally pronounced long, but short when followed by two consonants.

Here are some of the principal rules of pronunciation:

LETTER	ENGLISH EQUIVALENT	GERMAN EXAMPLE
Vowels		
a (short)	almost as the *u* in *cut*, not as the *a* in *cat*	**Mann** *man*; **kalt** *cold*
a (long)	as in *father*	**Vater** *father*; **Haar** *hair*
e (short)	as in *bed*	**Bett** *bed*; **wenn** *when*
e (long)	as in *they*	**Nebel** *fog*; **Feder** *pen*
i (short)	as in *pink*	**bitte** *please*; **Milch** *milk*
i (long)	as in *chief*	**ihn** *him*; **Kino** *cinema*
o (short)	as in *often*	**oft** *often*; **folgen** *to follow*
o (long)	as in *pole*	**gross** *big*; **Brot** *bread*

LETTER	ENGLISH EQUIVALENT	GERMAN EXAMPLE
u (short)	as in *put*, never as in *cut*	**Butter** *butter*; **und** *and*
u (long)	as in *blue*	**Stuhl** *chair*; **Stunde** *hour*
y	always as in *merry*	**typisch** *typical*

Modified vowels with umlaut(¨)

ä (short)	as *ea* in *head*	**Gepäck** *luggage*; **Männer** *men*
ä (long)	as in *pay*	**Mädchen** *girl*; **spät** *late*
ö (long)	as the *u* in turn	**schön** *beautiful*; **hören** *to hear*
ü (short)	as in the French *tu*, (no English equivalent)	**über** *over*; **Tür** *door*
ü (long)	as above but longer	**süss** *sweet*; **grün** *green*

Diphthongs

au	as in *now*	**Haus** *house*; **blau** *blue*
äu, eu	as in *toy*	**Häuser** *houses*; **Deutsch** *German*
ai, ei	as in *by*	**Kaiser** *emperor*; **Ei** *egg*
ee (also **eh**)	as in French *thé*, or halfway between *i* of *did* and *ay* of *day*	**Schnee** *snow*; **Mehl** *flour*
ie	as in *piece*	**tief** *deep*; **Liebe** *love*

Consonants that differ from the English:

c	as *k*	(rare in German)
ch	as in the Scots *loch*	**Buch** *book*; **auch** *also*

10

LETTER	ENGLISH EQUIVALENT	GERMAN EXAMPLE
d	at the end of a word is almost *t*	**Hand** *hand*; **Bad** *bath*
g	is hard except when a word ends in **ig**, when it is like **ch** above, but softer	**König** *king*; **lustig** *merry*
h	is pronounced before a vowel but is silent after one, and the vowel sound is lengthened	**Hecke** *hedge*; **gehen** *to go*
j	as the *y* of *yes*	**ja** *yes*; **jetzt** *now*
qu	as *kv*	**Quelle** *source*
s	as in *soft* at the end of a word or syllable	**Glas** *glass*; **Gastgeber** *host*
	as *z* at the beginning of a word or syllable	**sehen** *to see*; **Esel** *donkey*
	as *sh* at the beginning of a word where it is followed by *p* or *t*	**Spiel** *game*; **spät** *late*
sch	as *sh* in *shawl*	**Schule** *school*; **schade** *pity*
tio	as *tsio*	**Lektion** *lesson*

11

LETTER	ENGLISH EQUIVALENT	GERMAN EXAMPLE
th, dt	as *t*	**E***th***ik** *ethics*; **Stadt** *town*
v	as *f*	**Vogel** *bird*; **voll** *full*
w	as *v*	**warum** *why*; **Wasser** *water*
z	as the *ts* in boots	**Zahn** *tooth*; **zu** *to, too*

Note: the letter **ß** (ess-tsett) is sometimes written instead of **ss**, though the pronunciation is exactly the same e.g. **süß/süss**. In this book you wil find **ß** only in the Reading texts and in a very few isolated places where it is followed by another s.

THE GERMAN ALPHABET

Should you have to spell out names in German, remember that the pronunciation of individual letters differs from the English in many cases.

A ah **B** beh **C** tseh **D** deh **E** eh **F** eff **G** gay **H** hah **I** ee **J** yot **K** kah **L** ell **M** emm **N** enn **O** oh **P** peh **Q** koo **R** airr **S** ess **T** teh **U** oo **V** fow **W** veh **X** icks **Y** ipselon **Z** tsett.

KEY TO THE IMITATED PRONUNCIATION

Clearly, our system of imitation is only an approximation; it would be far better to listen to the recordings of this book. But if you have read the foregoing rules and bear in mind the notes below, you should be understood quite well.

ow   must be pronounced as in "cow", "how".

g   is always hard, as in "go" (never soft).

k   (*italic*) is guttural, as in the Scottish "loch" (not hard, as in "lock"). Often there is a slight slur that makes German words like "ich" sound more like "ish" but don't worry about it.

e   (*italic*) as in "open", "label".

ah   generally sounded long, but shorter and sharper when followed by two consonants.

EE   say "tree' with lips rounded for whistling; the terminal sound is that of the German ü.

12

EXPLANATION OF SOME GRAMMATICAL TERMS

Throughout this book we have used traditional grammatical terms. Readers unfamiliar with any of these should remember that they only serve to describe the way the language is used, and in most cases careful study of the examples will fully illustrate the point. To help you further, some of the terms most useful in a study of German are explained in the lessons themselves (see page references given below). Others may be briefly defined as follows:

adjective: word giving more information about a noun, e.g. a *red* book.
  possessive adjective: indicates possession. e.g. *his* boot, *our* house.
adverb: word giving more information about an action.
  —of time: tells when an action takes place. e.g. he *often* runs.
  —of manner: tells how an action takes place. e.g. he often runs *fast*.
  —of place: tells where an action takes place. e.g. he often runs *here* fast.
article:
  definite; *the*
  indefinitive: *a, an*
auxiliary verb: a verb used with another. e.g. she *will* come, she *must* come, she *has* come.
case:
  nominative: subject case (see p. 27)
  accusative: object case (see p. 27)
  dative: indirect object case (see p. 42)
  genitive: possessive case (see p. 74)
clause: group of words including a subject and a verb.
  main clause: one that can stand alone. e.g. *I saw her.*
  subordinate clause: one that cannot stand alone. e.g. I saw her *when I was crossing the street.*
comparative: form of adjective used in comparisons. In English usually ends in -*er*. e.g. Ann is *prettier* than Jane.
conjunction: word which joins one part of a sentence to another. e.g. We went to Germany *and* sailed up the Rhine.
  subordinate conjunction: begins a subordinate clause. e.g. I saw her *when* I was crossing the street.
imperative: an order e.g. *Come out! Stop talking!*
infinitive: form of a verb (one word in German) corresponding to English *to go, to ask.*
interrogative: question form.
irregular verb: one which does not conform to the common pattern of regular verbs.

13

past participle: form of verb used in perfect and other past tenses. e.g. I have *slept*, they had *played*.

prefix: addition to front of a word, e.g. *un*friendly.

preposition: word indicating relation of one thing to another. e.g. *over* the river, *with* my mother.

present participle: form of a verb ending in *-ing* in English. e.g. the *interesting* book.
—as in the example, it is often used as an adjective.

pronoun: a word that stands in place of a noun. See examples and English equivalents of:
personal pronouns—p.28
interrogative pronouns—p.79
reflexive pronouns—p. 28
relative pronouns—p. 89

reflexive verb: a verb relating to an action done to oneself followed in English (but preceded in German) by a **reflexive pronoun.** e.g. to *wash oneself*, they *enjoy themselves*.

regular verb: one which conforms to a common pattern.

relative pronoun: word referring to a noun already mentioned. e.g. the girl *who* has read the book *which* I bought.

stem: the part of the verb to which prefixes and endings are added. e.g. *frag-* is the stem of *fragen*.

subjunctive: a form of a verb necessary in certain contexts, much used in German, found in English—*were* he here (see p. 117)

subordinate: (see under **clause** and **conjunction**).

superlative: form of adjective used in comparisons to indicate the highest degree. In English it often ends in *-st* or *-est*. e.g. the *prettiest* dress.

tense: form of a verb indicating the time of an action—present, past, future, etc.

voice: passive or active (see p. 103).

14

Lesson One

The verb *to be* is one of the most important in any language, since it is an auxiliary—that is, one that can be used to help form the tenses of other verbs. So it is in German. Notice the alternative ('familiar') forms of the pronoun *you*; the use of these is explained in Lesson Six.

1 Sein—to be: PRESENT TENSE

singular	**ich bin**	I am
	du bist	you are (*familiar*)
	er ist	he is
	sie ist	she is
	es ist	it is
plural	**wir sind**	we are
	ihr seid	you are (*familiar*)
	Sie sind	you are
	sie sind	they are
negative	**ich bin nicht**	I am not
interrogative	**bin ich?**	am I?
neg. interrog.	**ist er nicht?**	is he not?

IMITATED PRONUNCIATION

sine; i*k* binn; doo bisst; air isst; see isst; ace isst; veer sinnt; eer site; see sinnt; see sinnt; i*k* binn ni*k*t; binn i*k*; isst air ni*k*t.
(Note that in this first presentation of the 'imitated pronunciation' we have given every word, repeatedly. We will continue to do so in the first two lessons, where verb forms are conjugated with their personal pronouns. After which, new words only will be imitated on their first appearance.)

EXERCISE I

1 Ich bin nicht.   2 Sie sind.   3 Ist er?   4 Es ist nicht.   5 Sind Sie nicht?   6 They are not.   7 Are we?   8 You are not.   9 Is she?   10 I am.

2   Sein—to be: PAST OR IMPERFECT TENSE

singular	**ich war**	I was
	du warst	you were (*fam.*)
	er war	he was
	sie war	she was
	es war	it was
plural	**wir waren**	we were
	ihr wart	you were (*fam.*)
	Sie waren	you were
	sie waren	they were
negative	**ich war nicht**	I was not
interrogative	**waren Sie?**	were you?
neg. interrog.	**waren sie nicht?**	were they not?

IMITATED PRONUNCIATION (2):

i*k* vahr; doo vahrst; air vahr; see vahr; ace vahr; veer vahr'-*en*; eer vahrt; see vahr'-*en*; see vahr'-*en*; i*k* vahr ni*k*t; vahr'-*en* see; vahr'-*en* see ni*k*t.

3   Questions are formed by placing the verb at the beginning of the sentence, or after the interrogative word **was, wo** etc.

EXERCISE II

1 Wir waren.   2 Sie waren nicht.   3 War er nicht?   4 Ich war nicht.   5 War sie?   6 They were not.   7 Were you?   8 He was not.   9 Were they not?   10 Were you not?

EXERCISE III

1 Wer ist hier?   2 Wo waren Sie?   3 Ich war hier.   4 Sind sie heute hier?   5 Nein, sie waren gestern hier.   6 Ist er heute

zu Hause? 7 Nein, er war gestern zu Hause. 8 Wie ist das?
9 Das ist schön. 10 Wo bin ich? 11 Is it small? 12 No, it
is not small. 13 Where were you yesterday? 14 I was at
home. 15 Is he upstairs? 16 No, he is not downstairs, he is
upstairs. 17 We were at home. 18 Are they here? 19
Yes, they are upstairs. 20 What is he? 21 How was that?

CONVERSATIONAL PRACTICE

Wo war das?	Where was that?
Wie ist das?	How is that?
Wer ist das?	Who is this?
Wo waren Sie gestern?	Where were you yesterday?
Ich war zu Hause.	I was at home.
Ist er hier?	Is he here?
Nein, er ist nicht hier.	No, he is not here.
Er ist dort.	He is there.
Ist es oben?	Is it upstairs?
Nein, es ist unten.	No, it is downstairs.

NEW WORDS

Lists of new words will be found at the end of each Lesson;
refer to them before doing each Exercise. You should also use a
dictionary in case there is need to look up the meaning of any
we have omitted to list.

ja	yes	**gross**	big, great
nein	no	**schön**	nice, fine
unten	downstairs	**klein**	small
oben	upstairs	**zu Hause**	at home,
das	that, this	**wer?**	who?
hier	here	**wo?**	where?
heute	today	**was?**	what?
gestern	yesterday	**wie?**	how?
dort	there		

IMITATED PRONUNCIATION

yah; nine; oonn'-ten; oh'-ben; duss; heer; hoy'-te; guess'-tern;
dort; grohs; shern; kline; tsoo how'-ze; vair; voh; vahss; vee.

17

Lesson Two

Regular verbs form their present tense as in the model given below. Note that the plural forms always end in **-en** (except after **ihr** which will be discussed in Lesson Six).

1 Machen—to make PRESENT TENSE

ich mache	I make
er macht	he makes
sie macht	she makes
es macht	it makes
wir machen	we make
Sie machen	you make
sie machen	they make

IMITATED PRONUNCIATION (1):

mah*k*'-*e*n; i*k* mah*k*'-*e*; air mah*k*t; see mah*k*t; ace mah*k*t; veer mah*k*'-*e*n; see mah*k*'-*e*n; see mah*k*'-*e*n.

When the stem of a verb (that part before the ending) terminates in **-d** or **-t**, the ending in the third person singular of the present tense is extended to **-et**. See page 6 of Hugo's "German Verbs Simplified".

2 Lernen—to learn PAST OR IMPERFECT TENSE

ich lernte	I learned
er lernte	he learned
sie lernte	she learned
es lernte	it learned
wir lernten	we learned

18

Sie lernten	you learned
sie lernten	they learned

IMITATED PRONUNCIATION (2):

i*k* lairn'-t*e*; air lairn'-t*e*; see lairn'-t*e*; ace lairn'-t*e*; veer lairn'-t*e*n; see lairn'-t*e*n; see lairn'-t*e*n.

EXERCISE I

1 Was machen Sie heute? 2 Wir spielten gestern. 3 Was kostet das? 4 Es kostet nichts. 5 Er verkaufte alles. 6 Ich machte es so. 7 I live here. 8 Where do you live? 9 What did he smoke? 10 I hear nothing. 11 What do they fetch?

3 **Haben**—to have PRESENT TENSE

ich habe	I have
er hat	he has
sie hat	she has
es hat	it has
wir haben	we have
Sie haben	you have
sie haben	they have

IMITATED PRONUNCIATION (3):

hah'-b*e*n; i*k* hah'-b*e*; air hahtt; see hahtt; ace hahtt; veer hah'-b*e*n; see hah'-b*e*n; see hah'-b*e*n.

4 **Haben**—to have: PAST OR IMPERFECT TENSE

ich hatte	I had
er hatte	he had
sie hatte	she had
es hatte	it had
wir hatten	we had
Sie hatten	you had
sie hatten	they had

19

IMITATED PRONUNCIATION (4):

haht'-ten; ik hahtt'-e; air hahtt'-e; see hahtt'-e; ace hahtt'-e;
veer haht'-ten; see haht'-ten; see haht'-ten.

EXERCISE II

1 Was lernen Sie? 2 Wir lernten Deutsch. 3 Hat sie viel
Geld? 4 Nein, sie hat nicht viel Geld. 5 Was hatte er?
6 Er hatte nichts. 7 Did you buy something? 8 No, I bought
nothing. 9 Who played? 10 We played yesterday. 11 Was
he here yesterday? 12 Yes, he was here yesterday.

5 Note that there is no equivalent in German of the English
use of the present participle (ending -*ing*) to form tenses, so
the translation is the same whether you say in English:

Are you learning? *or* Do you learn?	**Lernen Sie?**
I was asking *or* I asked	**Ich fragte.**
Did they play? *or* Were they playing?	**Spielten sie?**

6 In addition, note that certain everyday verbs form their
present tense irregularly in the 3rd person singular of the
present tense:

lesen	to read	er liest
sehen	to see	sie sieht
nehmen	to take	er nimmt
essen	to eat	sie isst
sprechen	to speak	er spricht
geben	to give	sie gibt
vergessen	to forget	er vergisst
schlafen	to sleep	er schläft
tragen	to carry, to wear	sie trägt
halten	to stop, to hold	er hält
verlassen	to leave	sie verlässt
fahren	to drive	er fährt

IMITATED PRONUNCIATION:

lay'-zen; air leest; say'-en; see seet; nay'-men; air nimmt;
ess'-en; see isst; shprek'-en, air sprikt; gay'-ben; see gibt; fair-

20

ghess'-en; air fair-gisst'; shlah'-fen; air shlayft; trahg'-en; see traygt; hahllt'-en; air helt; fair-lahss'-en; see fair-lesst'; fahr'-en; air fairt.

EXERCISE III

1 He speaks German well. 2 She reads a book. 3 He takes the letters. 4 She often forgets everything. 5 Does he sleep long?

NEW WORDS

All the verbs listed below are regular.

spielen	to play	**etwas**	something
lachen	to laugh	**Deutsch**	German
holen	to fetch	**Geld**	money
hören	to hear	**Auf Wieder-**	
wohnen	to live	**sehen**	goodbye
	(= reside)	**viel**	much, a lot (of)
rauchen	to smoke	**fragen**	to ask
kaufen	to buy	**gut**	good, well,
verkaufen	to sell	**oft**	often
kosten	to cost	**lange**	long (time)
nichts	not anything,	**die Briefe**	the letters
	nothing	**ein Buch**	a book
alles	all, everything		
so	so, like this, such		

IMITATED PRONUNCIATION:

shpeel'-en; lahk'-en; hohl'-en; her'-ren; voh'-nen; rowk'-en; kowf'-en; fair-kowf'-en; cost'-en; nikts; ahl'-les; so; et'-vahss; doytsh; gelt; owf veed'-er-zay-en; feel; frahg'-en; goot; oft; lahng'-e; dee breef'-e; ine book.

Lesson Three

1 The definite article, *the*, is affected in German by the gender of the noun it precedes. That is, it changes according to whether the noun is masculine, feminine or neuter. It also changes between singular and plural nouns. Consider 50% of all nouns to be masculine, with the rest divided 2 to 1 approximately between feminine and neuter.

der	*masculine (m)*	**der Mann**	the man
die	*feminine (f)*	**die Frau**	the woman
das	*neuter (n)*	**das Kind**	the child
die	*m/f/n plural (pl)*		

IMITATED PRONUNCIATION (1):

der; dee; duss; dee; der mahnn; dee frow; duss kint; dee men'-ner; dee frow'-en; dee kin'-der.

The best advice is to learn the article with each noun as it occurs. (Notice, by the way, that all German nouns begin with a capital letter.) Here are some rules to help you remember the genders:

2 Masculine nouns—in addition to the bulk—are:

(i) Days, months and seasons.

der Sonntag	Sunday
der Montag	Monday
der Dienstag	Tuesday
der Mittwoch	Wednesday
der Donnerstag	Thursday
der Freitag	Friday

| der Samstag | Saturday |
| der Sonnabend | Saturday (in North Germany) | ✗ |

der Januar	January
der Februar	February
der März	March
der April	April
der Mai	May
der Juni	June
der Juli	July
der August	August
der September	September
der Oktober	October
der November	November
der Dezember	December

der Frühling	Spring
der Sommer	Summer
der Herbst	Autumn
der Winter	Winter

IMITATED PRONUNCIATION (2, i):

sonn'-tahg; mohn'-tahg; deens'-tahg; mit'-vok; donn'-ers-
tahg; fry'-tahg; sonn'-ah-bent; sahms'-tahg; yahn'-oo-ahr;
fay'-broo-ahr; mairts; ahp-ril'; my; yoo'-nee; yoo'-lee; ow-
goost'; sept-em-ber; oct-o'-ber; noh-vem'-ber; day-tsem'-ber;
frEE'-ling; somm'-er; hairpst; vint'-er.

(ii) Masculine also: some metals and most precious stones.

der Stahl	the steel
der Marmor	the marble
der Diamant	the diamond
der Smaragd	the emerald
der Rubin	the ruby

(iii) Words ending in **-ig, -ich, -ing** and **-ling** are also
masculine:

| der König | the king |
| der Käfig | the cage |

23

der Rettich	the radish
der Teppich	the carpet
der Sperling	the sparrow
der Ring	the ring

IMITATED PRONUNCIATION (2, ii/iii):

stahll; marm'-ohr; dee-ah-mahnt'; smah-rahkt;' roob-een';
kern'-i*k*; kay'- fi*k*; ret'-ti*k*; tep'-pi*k*; shpairr'-ling; ring.

3 Feminine nouns are those which end in **-e, -tion, -tät, -schaft, -heit, -keit** and **-ung:**

die Lampe	the lamp
die Nation	the nation
die Universität	the university
die Mannschaft	the team
die Gesundheit	the health
die Freundlichkeit	the kindness
die Rechnung	the bill, invoice

IMITATED PRONUNCIATION (3):

lahmp'-*e*; nah-tse-ohn'; oonn-e-vair-se-tayt; mahn'-shafft; ge-
zoont'- hite; froynt'-lik-kite; re*k*'-noong.

4 Neuter nouns are

(i) Those which end in **-o,** with some exceptions. Learn the exceptions as they occur.

das Auto	the car
das Kino	the cinema
das Büro	the office

(ii) Some nouns of foreign origin.

das Hotel	the hotel
das Theater	the theatre
das Restaurant	the restaurant

24

(iii) Nouns which end in **-nis** and **-zeug.**

das Ereignis	the occurrence
das Strickzeug	the knitting
das Spielzeug	the toy
das Ergebnis	the result

(iv) Nouns ending in **-chen** or **-lein,** which make a word diminutive and convert any noun into a neuter noun.

das Mädchen	the girl
das Fräulein	the Miss ('little woman')

IMITATED PRONUNCIATION (4):

ow'-toh; keen'-oh; ʙᴇᴇʀ'-oh; ho-tell'; tay-aht'-*er*; rest-oh-rant'; air-i'-gniss; shtrick'-tsoyk; shpeel'-tsoyk; air-gape'-niss; mait'-*ke*n; froy'-line.

5 The indefinite article, *a*, changes according to the gender of the noun it precedes (just like the definite article does):

ein	*masculine* (m)	**ein Tisch**	a table
eine	*feminine* (f)	**eine Lampe**	a lamp
ein	*neuter* (n)	**ein Fenster**	a window

IMITATED PRONUNCIATION (5): ine; i'-n*e*; ine; ine tish; i'-n*e* lahm'-p*e*; ine fenst'-er.

6 The expression *not any, not a* or *no* in front of a noun must be translated by **kein** (*m* and *n*) or **keine** (*f* and *pl*):

Das ist kein Tisch, das ist ein Stuhl.
This is not a table, this is a chair.
Haben Sie kein Geld?
Have you no money?
Nein, ich habe kein Geld.
No, I have no money.
Wir haben keine Zeit.
We have no time.

CONVERSATIONAL PRACTICE

Rauchen wir eine Zigarette?	Are we smoking a cigarette?
Nein, wir rauchen eine Zigarre.	No, we are smoking a cigar.
Hatten Sie gestern viel Arbeit?	Did you have much work yesterday?
Ja, ich hatte viel Arbeit.	Yes, I had much work.
Was hört er?	What is he listening to?
Er hört das Konzert.	He is listening to the concert.
Wer hat das Buch?	Who has the book?
Ich habe das Buch.	I have the book.
Wo ist der Tisch?	Where is the table?
Warum sind Sie nicht fertig?	Why are you not ready?
Wo ist das Telefon?	Where is the telephone?

NEW WORDS

die Arbeit	the work
die Zeit	the time
das Geld	the money
das Konzert	the concert
die Zigarette	the cigarette
die Zigarre	the cigar
der Tisch	the table
der Stuhl	the stool
das Telefon	the telephone
fertig	ready
warum	why
sagen	to say

IMITATED PRONUNCIATION:

kine; kine'-*e*; ahr'-bite; tsite; gelt; kon-tsairt'; tsee-gah-ret'-*e*; tsee-gahrr'-*e*; tish; shtool; tay'-l*e*-fohn; fairt'-ik; vah-roomm'; sahg'-*e*n.

26

Lesson Four

A sentence must have—in addition to a verb—a subject, and it can have an object. In *the house is big*, the subject is *house*; in *he has a big house*, the object is *house*. In German, the definite or indefinite article changes—but only before a masculine singular noun—according to whether the subject case (nominative) or object case (accusative) is needed. Note in the examples below how the feminine and neuter articles do not change.

1 *Nominative*

	the		a, an	
	der (*m*)		**ein** (*m*)	
	die (*f*)		**eine** (*f*)	
	das (*n*)		**ein** (*n*)	

der Wagen	= **er ist gross**	it is big
die Tasche	= **sie ist schön**	it is beautiful
das Buch	= **es ist blau**	it is blue

2 *Accusative*

	the		a, an	
	den (*m*)		**einen** (*m*)	
	die (*f*)		**eine** (*f*)	
	das (*n*)		**ein** (*n*)	

Bestellen Sie den Wagen?	Do you order the car?
Ja, ich bestelle ihn.	Yes, I order it.
Haben Sie einen Brief?	Have you a letter?

IMITATED PRONUNCIATION (1, 2):

der; dee; duss; ine; ine'-*e*; ine; den; dee; duss; ine'-*en*; ine'-*e*; ine.

27

EXERCISE I

1 Where is the car? 2 It is here. 3 Have you a ballpen?
4 Yes, I have one. 5 Where is the clock? 6 It is here. 7
Have you the postcard? 8 Yes, I have it. 9 Please order a
taxi. 10 It is coming immediately. 11 I would like a newspaper. 12 How much is it? 13 How much does the pencil
cost? 14 It costs 30 Pf.

3 List of Pronouns

NOMINATIVE		ACCUSATIVE		REFLEXIVE	
ich	I	**mich**	me	**mich**	myself
er	he	**ihn**	him	**sich**	himself
sie	she	**sie**	her	**sich**	herself
es	it	**es**	it	**sich**	itself
wir	we	**uns**	us	**uns**	ourselves
Sie	you	**Sie**	you	**sich**	yourself
					yourselves
sie	they	**sie**	them	**sich**	themselves

4 Possessive Adjectives

mein	my
sein	his
ihr	her
sein	its
unser	our
Ihr	your
ihr	their

IMITATED PRONUNCIATION (3, 4):

i*k*; air; see; ace; veer; see; see; mi*k*; een; see; ace; oonss; see;
see; mi*k*; si*k*; si*k*; si*k*; oonss; si*k*; si*k*; mine; sine; eer; sine;
oon'-ser; eer; eer.

EXERCISE II

1 Do you see him? 2 No, I do not see him. 3 I am buying a
pencil. 4 Is this your office? 5 Yes, it is my office. 6 Here

is our table.   7 Where is it?   8 Do you know his secretary?
9 No, I do not know her.   10 When do you want the car?
11 I would like it immediately.

5   Reflexive verbs

to shave	**sich rasieren**
to meet	**sich treffen**
to wash oneself	**sich waschen**
to converse	**sich unterhalten**
to be pleased	**sich freuen**
to look forward to	**sich freuen auf**
to sit oneself down	**sich setzen**
to feel	**sich fühlen**

IMITATED PRONUNCIATION:

si*k* rahz-eer'-en; si*k* tref'-fen; si*k* vahsh'-en; si*k* oonn'-ter-
hahlt-en; si*k* froy'-en; si*k* froy'-en owf; si*k* setz'-en; si*k* fEEl'-en.

EXERCISE III

1 Where are you going to sit?   2 I am sitting here.   3 How
do you feel?   4 I am feeling well.   5 Is he washing himself?
6 Yes, he is washing himself.   7 Is he pleased?   8 Yes, he is
pleased.   9 Is she looking forward to the holidays?   10 Yes,
she is looking forward to them.   11 Did you pay the bill?
12 No, I did not pay it.   13 They converse for a long time.

NEW WORDS

der Brief	the letter
der Kugel-	
schreiber	the ballpen
der Bleistift	the pencil
das Taxi	the taxi
das Büro	the office
die Sekretärin	the secretary

29

die Uhr	the watch, clock
die Postkarte	the postcard
die Zeitung	the newspaper
der Wagen	the car
die Zeit	the time
die Ferien	the holidays
bestellen	to order
kennen	to know (people)
besuchen	to visit
ich möchte	I would like
sofort	immediately
wieviel	how much
sehen	to see

IMITATED PRONUNCIATION:

breef; koog'-el-shry-ber; bly'-shtift; taxi; bEEr-oh'; seck-re-tair'-een; oohr; posst'-kart-e; tsy'-toong; vahg'-en; tsite; fair'-yen; be-shtel'-oong; ken'-en; be-sook'-en; ik merk'-te; so-fort'; vee'-feel; say'-en.

Lesson Five

1 To form the **perfect tense** of most verbs we use **haben** as in English (for exceptions see Lesson 9): *I have played*. This is followed by the past participle, which in regular verbs is formed by putting **ge-** before and **-t** or **-et** after the stem.

leben	to live	**wir haben**	*gelebt*
zählen	to count	**er hat**	*gezählt*
machen	to make	**ich habe**	*gemacht*
spielen	to play	**sie haben**	*gespielt*
kaufen	to buy	**Sie haben**	*gekauft*
warten	to wait	**sie hat**	*gewartet*
haben	to have	**er hat**	*gehabt*

The past participle always goes to the end of the sentence or the clause, whichever comes first.

2 Verbs with prefixes do not take **ge-**, but they do end in **-t**.

besuchen	to visit	**er hat mich** *besucht*
verkaufen	to sell	**wir haben das Haus** *verkauft*
erzählen	to tell, relate	**sie hat uns eine Geschichte** *erzählt*
entschuldigen	to excuse	**Sie haben ihn** *entschuldigt*
wiederholen	to repeat	**ich habe die Übung** *wiederholt*
missbrauchen	to misuse	**sie haben das Gesetz** *missbraucht*

lay'-ben; ge-laybt'; tsay'-len; ge-tsaylt'; mahk'-en; ge-mahkt'; shpee'-len; ge-shpeelt'; kow'-fen; ge-kowft'; vahr'-ten; ge-vahrt'-et; hah'-ben; ge-hahbt'; be-sook'-en; be-sookt'; fair-kow'-fen; fair-kowft'; airt-say'-len; airt-saylt'; ent-shooll'-dig-en; ent-shooll'-digt; veed-er-hohl'-en; veed-er-holt'; miss-browk'-en; miss-browkt'.

3 Many German verbs are separable. They form one word in the infinitive but separate in the present and imperfect tenses.

e.g. **ausgehen**	to go out
ich gehe aus	I go out
er holte es ab	he fetched it

4 Verbs which are separable put **ge-** in between prefix and verb. Separable verbs always have a stressed prefix.

abholen	to collect	**sie hat ihn *abgeholt***
einkaufen	to shop	**ich habe viel *eingekauft***
aufführen	to perform	**sie haben ein Theater-stück *aufgeführt***

5 Verbs which end in **-ieren** do not take **ge-** in the perfect tense.

telefonieren	to phone	**sie hat gestern morgen *telefoniert***
probieren	to try, to taste	**ich habe das Essen *probiert***
studieren	to study	**wir haben Deutsch *studiert***
reparieren	to repair	**Sie haben die Schuhe *repariert***

owss'-gay-en; ahp'-hoh-len; ahp-ge-hohlt'; ine'-kow-fen; ine-ge-kowft'; owf'-fEER-en; owf-ge-fEErt'; tay-lay-fohn-eer'-en; tay-lay-fohn-eerrt'; pro-beer'-en; pro-beert'; shtoo-deer'-en; shtoo-deert'; rep-ah-reer'-en; rep-ah-reert'.

6 In conversation the tendency is to use the perfect tense rather then the imperfect, so in most cases it is advisable to translate both the English perfect and simple past by the German perfect.

e.g. I have bought a dress ⎱ **ich habe ein Kleid gekauft**
    I bought a dress ⎰

EXERCISE I

1 Have you bought a carpet? 2 No, I have not bought a carpet. 3 Has he ordered a table? 4 Yes, the table is ordered. 5 Have they sold the ring? 6 Yes, they have sold the ring. 7 The teacher has repeated the question.

7 Word Order

When a word other than the subject begins a sentence the word order must be inverted, i.e. the verb must be the second idea in the sentence. The stressed point (such as the time factor) usually begins a sentence.

e.g. heute **kommt** er früh nach Hause
    gestern **hat** er lange auf mich gewartet

EXERCISE II

1 In spring the flowers bloom. 2 Has she enough money to pay the bill? 3 My friend (has) phoned yesterday. 4 On Sunday we (have) visited the hotel. 5 Where have you been living? 6 In England? 7 Yes, I have been living in England.

Note the sentences with the bracket indicate that in English one uses the imperfect, whereas in German the perfect tense must be used.

33

Eine kurze Geschichte—A short story

Herr Schulz kommt heute früh nach Hause. Er hatte heute wenig Arbeit. Seine Frau und die Kinder haben schon auf ihn gewartet. Sie sind alle hungrig. Sie hat schon das Essen vorbereitet. Heute gibt es eine Suppe, einen Braten und Gemüse. Zum Schluss hat sie eine Schüssel Obst serviert. Den Abend verbringt die Familie zu Hause. Herr Schulz liest eine Zeitung und seine Frau strickt einen Pullover. Die Kinder machen ihre Schulaufgaben und dann setzen sie sich vor den Fernsehapparat und sehen einen Film. Herr Schulz sieht nicht fern, er arbeitet noch etwas und dann gehen sie alle zu Bett. Sie sind sehr müde.

VOCABULARY TO THE STORY

wenig	little
schon	already
hungrig	hungry
die Suppe	the soup
der Braten	the roast
das Gemüse	the vegetable
die Schüssel	the bowl, dish
das Obst	the fruit
stricken	to knit
der Pullover	the pullover
die Schulaufgaben	the homework
der Fernsehapparat	the television
fernsehen	to watch T.V.
verbringen (*irreg.*)	to spend (time)
dann	then
zu Bett	(to go) to bed
müde	tired

IMITATED PRONUNCIATION:

vain'-i*k*; shohn; hoong'-ri*k*; soopp'-*e*; brah'ten; ge-mEEz'-*e*; shEE'-s*e*ll; ohpst; strick'-*e*n; pool'-oh-v*e*r; shool'-owf-gah-b*e*n; fairn'-zay-ahp-pahr-rat'; fairn'-zay-*e*n; fair-bring'-*e*n; dahnn; tsoo bett; mEED'-*e*.

CONVERSATIONAL PRACTICE

Haben Sie den Preis bezahlt?	Have you paid the price?
Nein, es war zu teuer.	No it was too expensive.
Haben Sie Feuer? Ich möchte eine Zigarette rauchen.	Have you a light? I would like to smoke a cigarette.
Wo ist das Telefon?	Where is the telephone?
Es ist dort.	It is there.
Wann kommt der Zug an?	When does the train arrive?
Um elf Uhr auf Bahnsteig zwei.	At eleven o'clock on platform two
Auf wen haben Sie gewartet?	For whom have you been waiting?
Ich habe auf sie gewartet.	I have been waiting for her.
Gibt es hier eine deutsche Zeitung?	Can I get a German paper here?
Nein, hier gibt es keine.	No, there are none available here.

NEW WORDS

die Geschichte	the story	**im Frühling**	in spring
die Übung	the exercise	**am Sonntag**	on Sunday
das Gesetz	the law	**die Frage**	the question
das Essen	the food, the meal	**die Blumen**	the flowers
		blühen	to bloom
die Schuhe	the shoes	**vorbereiten**	to prepare
die Karten	the playing cards	**früh**	early

IMITATED PRONUNCIATION:

ge-shic*k*t'-*e*; EEb'-oong; ge-setz'; ess'-*e*n; shoo'-*e*; kahr'-t*e*n; im froy'-ling; am sonn'-tahg; frah'-ge; bloom'-*e*n; blEE'-*e*n; for'-be-ry-t*e*n; froy.

35

Lesson Six

1 All **auxiliary verbs** are irregular in the singular and they force the verb in the infinitive to the end of the clause or the sentence, whichever comes first.

müssen   *to have to, must*

ich muss	I must	**wir müssen**	we must
er muss	he must	**Sie müssen**	you must
sie muss	she must	**sie müssen**	they must
es muss	it must		

können   *to be able to, can*

ich kann	I can	**wir können**	we can
er kann	he can	**Sie können**	you can
sie kann	she can	**sie können**	they can
es kann	it can		

dürfen   *to be allowed to, may*

ich darf	I may	**wir dürfen**	we may
er darf	he may	**Sie dürfen**	you may
sie darf	she may	**sie dürfen**	they may
es darf	it may		

wollen   *want to, will*

ich will	I want to	**wir wollen**	we want to
er will	he wants to	**Sie wollen**	you want to
sie will	she wants to	**sie wollen**	they want to
es will	it wants to		

mögen   *to like to, like*

ich mag	I like	**wir mögen**	we like
er mag	he likes	**Sie mögen**	you like

sie mag	she likes	**sie mögen**	they like
es mag	it likes		
sollen	*ought to, shall*		
ich soll	I shall	**wir sollen**	we shall
er soll	he shall	**Sie sollen**	you shall
sie soll	she shall	**sie sollen**	they shall
es soll	it shall		

e.g. **Ich muss viel arbeiten.**
I must work hard.
Darf ich Sie begleiten?
May I accompany you?
Wir mögen diesen Kaffee nicht.
We do not like this coffee.
Er kann Deutsch.
He can speak German.
Sollen wir Sie heute abend abholen?
Shall we fetch you this evening?

IMITATED PRONUNCIATION:

mEESS'-en; kern'-en; dEErf'-en; voll'-en; merg'-en; sol'-en.

2 In German, contrary to English, an auxiliary verb can be used without another verb when the meaning is obvious.

e.g. **Können Sie Deutsch?**
Can you speak German?
Ja, ich kann Deutsch.
Yes, I can.

Exercise I

1 Can you read this? 2 Yes, I can. 3 Does he want to go home? 4 No, he wants to stay here. 5 Must you sell the flat? 6 Yes, unfortunately I have to sell it. 7 We would like a cup of coffee. 8 Does she want to come on Sunday? 9 No, she wants to come on Saturday.

EXERCISE II

1 May he open the window? 2 Of course he may. 3 She has to prepare the dinner. 4 It must be ready by 7 o'clock. 5 Can you change this banknote? 6 No, I cannot, I have no change.

3 The **imperative** is formed like a question except that the intonation of the voice remains on the same level, whereas in a question the voice goes up.

e.g. **Kommen Sie bitte herein!**   *Please come in.*
    Gehen Sie jetzt bitte hinaus!   *Please leave.*

Sie is the polite form of address and it is advisable to stick to this in everyday life. However, between friends and members of one's own family, also when addressing children and animals, one uses **du** in the singular and **ihr** in the plural.

e.g. Singular   *Plural*
    du spielst   **ihr spielt**
    du lernst   **ihr lernt**
    du gibst   **ihr gebt**

Please note that **-st** is always added to the verb in the **du** form; the **ihr** form of the verb ends in **-t**, or **-et** if the **-t** cannot be pronounced properly. But the **du** form loses the **-st** in the Imperative and neither form has a pronoun in the imperative:

e.g. Singular   *Plural*
    komm her!   **kommt her!**
    geh hinaus!   **geht hinaus!**

The auxiliary verbs obey the same rules and add **-st** to the **du** form and **-t** to the **ihr** form:
    du darfst   **ihr dürft**
    du kannst   **ihr könnt**

EXERCISE III

1 Can you (*du*) visit me to-morrow? 2 Yes, I can come. 3 Buy (*du*) the house! 4 Learn (*ihr*) German! 5 Ask (*Sie*) him! 6 Sleep (*Sie*) well!

5 Cardinal Numbers

1	eins
2	zwei
3	drei
4	vier
5	fünf
6	sechs
7	sieben
8	acht
9	neun
10	zehn
11	elf
12	zwölf
13	dreizehn
14	vierzehn
15	fünfzehn
16	sechzehn
17	siebzehn
18	achtzehn
19	neunzehn
20	zwanzig
21	einundzwanzig
30	dreissig
32	zweiunddreissig
40	vierzig
43	dreiundvierzig
50	fünfzig
54	vierundfünfzig
60	sechzig
65	fünfundsechzig
70	siebzig
76	sechsundsiebzig
80	achtzig
87	siebenundachtzig
90	neunzig
98	achtundneunzig
99	neunundneunzig
100	hundert

but; 116 **hundertsechzehn** (note no **und** between **hundert** and the other figures).

IMITATED PRONUNCIATION:

ines; tsvy; dry; feer; fᴇᴇnf; sex; see'-b*e*n; ah*k*t; noyn; tsayn; elf; tsverlf; dry'-tsayn; feer'-tsayn; fᴇᴇnf'-tsayn; se*k*'-tsayn; seep'-tsayn; ah*k*'-tsayn; noyn'-tsayn; tsvahn'-tsi*k*; iné-oont-tsvahn-tsi*k*; dry'-si*k*; tsvy'-oont-dry-si*k*; feer'-tsi*k*; dry'-oont-feer-tsi*k*; fᴇᴇnf'-tsi*k*; feer'-oont-fᴇᴇnf-tsi*k*; sex-*s*i*k*; fᴇᴇnf'-oont-sex-si*k*; seep'-tsi*k*; sex'-oont-seep-tsi*k*; ah*k*'-tsi*k*; see'-b*e*n-oont-ah*k*-tsi*k*; noyn'-tsi*k*; ah*k*t'-oont-noyn-tsi*k*; noyn'-oont-noyn-tsi*k*; hoonn'-dert; hoonn'-dert-se*k*-tsayn.

6   Expressions of Time

Perhaps the most important point to note is how to say "half past" an hour in German. Whereas in English we always use the hour just past (*ten thirty, half past ten, half ten*), the German expression uses the hour that is coming next—as may be seen from the example below.

10^{00}	**zehn Uhr**
10^{05}	**fünf Minuten nach zehn**
10^{10}	**zehn Minuten nach zehn**
10^{15}	**viertel nach zehn**
10^{20}	**zwanzig Minuten nach zehn** *or* **zehn vor halb elf**
10^{25}	**fünf Minuten vor halb elf**
10^{30}	**halb elf**
10^{35}	**fünf Minuten nach halb elf**
10^{40}	**zehn Minuten nach halb elf** *or* **zwanzig Minuten vor elf**
10^{45}	**viertel vor elf**
10^{50}	**zehn Minuten vor elf**
10^{55}	**fünf Minuten vor elf**
11^{00}	**elf Uhr**

Wieviel Uhr ist es?	What time is it?
Es ist zehn Uhr.	It is ten o'clock.

Um drei Uhr.	At three o'clock.
Morgens, abends.	In the morning, in the evening.
Nach fünf nachmittags ist es abends.	After five p.m. it is considered to be evening.

Note the above use of *nachmittags* ("after noon"). It is also advisable to use the 24-hour clock for appointments and so on:

$$1^{30} = 13^{30} \quad \textbf{dreizehn Uhr dreissig}$$

7 Currency and **measurements** are always expressed in the singular, in German:

Das kostet 100 Mark.
Das Büro ist 10 Meter lang.

NEW WORDS

eine Tasse Kaffee	a cup of coffee
die Wohnung	the flat
um sieben Uhr	by 7 o'clock
am Samstag	on Saturday
nach Hause gehen	to go home
kein Kleingeld	no change
die Banknote *or* **der Geldschein**	the banknote
das Geld	the money
die Uhr	the clock
die Stunde	the hour
wechseln	to change
bleiben	to stay
leider	unfortunately

IMITATED PRONUNCIATION:

ine'-*e* tahss'-*e* kahff'-ay; voh'-noong; oom see'-b*e*n oohr; am sahms'-tahg; nah*k* how'-s*e* gay'-*e*n; kine kline'-gelt; bahnk'-noht-*e*; gelt'-shine; gelt; oohr; shtoon'-d*e*; vex'-*e*ln; bly'-b*e*n; ly'-d*e*r.

Lesson Seven

The dative case

The indirect object in English is normally preceded by *to* or *for*. In *I gave the book to her,* the indirect object is *her*. (Sometimes of course *to* is omitted as in *I gave her the book*.)
In German the indirect object is indicated by use of the dative case.

1 The definite articles change from

> **der** to **dem** (*m*)   **die** to **der**(*f*)   **das** to **dem** (*n*)
> **die** to **den** (*pl.*)

Thus the list of definite articles is as follows;

	MASC.	FEM.	NEUT.	PLUR.
Nom.	**der**	**die**	**das**	**die**
Acc.	**den**	**die**	**das**	**die**
Dat.	**dem**	**der**	**dem**	**den (n)**

The (**n**) in the dative plural indicates that an **n** must be added to all plural nouns unless they end in **n** already (see Lesson 10).

2 The indefinite articles change similarly:

Nom.	**ein**	**eine**	**ein**	**keine**
Acc.	**einen**	**eine**	**ein**	**keine**
Dat.	**einem**	**einer**	**einem**	**keinen**

3 The dative and accusative of pronouns are as follows:

	ACCUSATIVE		DATIVE	
Singular	**mich**	me	**mir**	to me
	dich	you *(fam)*	**dir**	to you *(fam)*
	ihn	him	**ihm**	to him
	sie	her	**ihr**	to her
	es	it	**ihm**	to it
Plural	**uns**	us	**uns**	to us
	euch	you *(fam)*	**euch**	to you *(fam)*
	Sie	you	**Ihnen**	to you
	sie	them	**ihnen**	to them

IMITATED PRONUNCIATION (1, 2, 3):

dair, dem; dee, dair; duss, dem; dee, den; ine, ine'-*en*,.ine'-*em*;
ine'-*e*, ine'-*er*; kine'-*e*, kine'-*en*; mi*k*, di*k*, een, see, ace, oonss,
oy*k*, see; meer, deer, eem, eer, een'-*en*.

4 In the dative case we add the appropriate endings to the
possessive adjectives thus:

> **er gibt seiner Tochter ein Stück Schokolade**
> **er gibt es seiner Tochter**

5 Note that:

(*a*) in the case of two nouns the dative comes before the
accusative

(*b*) in the case of two pronouns the accusative comes before the
dative

(*c*) in the case of pronoun and noun—the pronoun comes before
the noun whatever the case.

e.g. **Er diktiert seiner Sekretärin einen Brief.**
He dictates a letter to his secretary.
Ja, ich gebe es ihm.
Yes, I give it to him.
Gibst du ihm das Buch?
Do you give him the book?

43

6 Prepositions which take the accusative

gegen	against	für	for
um	at, round	durch	through
entlang*	along	ohne	without

7 Prepositions which take the dative

aus	out of	seit	since
bei	at, near (place)	gegenüber**	opposite
mit	with	von	of, from
nach	after	zu	to

IMITATED PRONUNCIATION (6, 7):

gay'-gen, oomm, ent-lahng', fEEr, doohrk, oh'-ne; owss, by, mit, nah*k*, site, fon, gay'-gen-EEb-er.

Examples   THE ACCUSATIVE

Er kommt gegen acht Uhr. (*time*)
He comes at about eight o'clock.
Sie lehnt gegen den Stuhl.
She is leaning against the chair.
Wir sitzen um den Tisch.
We are sitting around the table.
Ich gehe den Fluss entlang.
I am walking along the river.
Ist das Geschenk für mich?
Is the present for me?
Der Vater kommt ohne seinen Sohn.
The father comes without his son.
Du gehst durch den Garten spazieren.
You are walking through the garden.

---

* **entlang** is used after the noun
** **gegenüber** is used after the noun

Examples <small>THE DATIVE</small>

Das Kind kommt aus der Schule.
The child is coming out of school.
Sie wohnt bei ihren Eltern.
She lives with her parents.
Kommst du mit mir?
Are you coming with me?
Er lernt Deutsch seit einigen Monaten.
He has been learning German for a few months.
Die Idee kommt von seinem Chef.
The idea is his boss's (originates from his boss.)
Das Büro ist dem Bahnhof gegenüber.
The office is opposite the station.

EXERCISE I

1 The lady travels with her husband to Germany.   2 We do
not live with him.   3 The official gives the foreigner a piece
of paper.   4 He gives me his address.   5 Fetch him the newspaper.   6 Show me your passport.

8   The following verbs take the dative case.

REGULAR

danken	to thank
erlauben	to allow
folgen	to follow
passen	to suit
antworten	to answer
gehören	to belong
schicken	to send
mitteilen	to inform
gratulieren	to congratulate
zeigen	to show

IRREGULAR

verbieten	to forbid
befehlen	to command
widersprechen	to contradict
versprechen	to promise
helfen	to help
leihen	to lend
bringen	to bring
verzeihen	to forgive, to excuse

9 The following verbs, used impersonally, also take the dative case:

REGULAR

schmecken	to taste	**Das schmeckt mir**
		I like the taste of that
fehlen an	to lack	**Es fehlt ihm an Geld**
		He's short of money
dauern	to last	**Es dauerte ihm zu lange**
		It was too long for him (to wait)

IRREGULAR

leid tun	to be sorry	**es tut mir leid**	I am sorry
gelingen	to succeed	**es gelingt mir**	I succeed
gefallen	to please	**es gefällt mir**	it pleases me
einfallen	to occur	**es fällt mir ein**	it occurs to me
scheinen	to seem	**es scheint mir**	it seems to me

EXERCISE II

1 Do you see him? 2 Yes, I can see him. 3 What are you buying yourself? 4 I am buying myself a coat. 5 Are you showing her the photos? 6 Yes, I am showing them to her. 7 Does he help you with your work? 8 No, he does not help me. 9 Are you sorry? 10 Yes, I am very sorry.

NEW WORDS

das Stück Schokolade	the piece of chocolate
der Garten	the garden
die Eltern	the parents
der Mann	(*in this case*) the husband
die Adresse	the address
der Pass	the passport
das Kleid	the dress
der Mantel	the coat
der Anzug	the suit (*man's*)
der Beamte	the official
der Ausländer	the foreigner
der Zettel	the piece of paper
das Photo	the photo
lehnen	to lean
holen	to collect, to fetch
abholen	to collect, to fetch (somebody)
reisen	to travel
einige	some (*plural*)
etwas	something

IMITATED PRONUNCIATION:

shtEECk shoh-koh-lahd'-*e*; gahrt'-*e*n; el'-t*e*rn; mahnn; ah-dress'-*e*; pahss; klite; mahnn'-t*e*l; ahn'-tsook; b*e*-ahm'-t*e*; owss'-len-d*e*r; tset'-*e*l; foh'-toh; lay'-n*e*n; hoh'-l*e*n; ahp'-hoh-l*e*n; ry'-s*e*n; ine'-ig-*e*; et'-vahss.

From this point onwards we will no longer supply the imitated pronunciation of German words unless they completely ignore the usual rules. You should now be at a stage where the pronunciation is no problem—if it is, then you must revise the early paragraphs or listen closely to our recordings of the text, if you have them.

Lesson Eight

1 Irregular verbs form their **imperfect tense** as in the following examples:

gehen *to go*

ich ging	I went	**wir gingen**	we went
du gingst	you went	**ihr gingt**	you went
er ging	he went	**Sie gingen**	you went
sie ging	she went	**sie gingen**	they went
es ging	it went		

kommen *to come*

ich kam	I came	**wir kamen**	we came
du kamst	you came	**ihr kamt**	you came
er kam	he came	**Sie kamen**	you came
sie kam	she came	**sie kamen**	they came
es kam	it came		

(Note that no additional endings are added except in the **du** form which takes **-st**; the plural ending is **-en** except in the **ihr** form which takes a **-t** as in the present tense.)

As there are no specific rules for the irregular verbs, it is advisable to learn them as they occur. We would refer you to *Hugo's German Verbs Simplified.*

2 We have already explained in Lesson Five how the perfect tense is used in conversation, but the imperfect is useful in relating a story which happened in the past and is concluded.

48

EXERCISE I (Use the imperfect)

1 Did you see the accident? 2 No, I did not see it. 3 Did she write a letter to her friend? 4 Yes, she wrote to him. 5 Did you go to the cinema last night? 6 No, we did not go. 7 Did he manage to repair the car? 8 Yes, the car is repaired. 9 Did you phone your girlfriend? 10 Yes, but she was not at home.

Eine kurze Geschichte—*A short story*

Herr Maier hatte gestern einen Autounfall. Ein Fahrer stiess mit ihm in der Einbahnstrasse zusammen. Der Fahrer war falsch eingebogen. Zuerst war Herr Maier sehr ärgerlich. Er wollte nämlich schnell noch ein paar Besorgungen machen und dann seine Frau in der Stadt treffen. Beide Fahrer tauschten ihre Adressen aus. Sie wollten sich wieder mit einander in Verbindung setzen. Herr Maier ging zu seiner Garage und bat Herrn Schulz den Wagen zu reparieren. Der versprach den Wagen so bald wie möglich fertig zu haben. Herr Maier rief ein Taxi und ging ins Café um seine Frau zu treffen.

3 The imperfect of all auxiliary verbs is formed regularly, except that those with an umlaut lose it in the imperfect.

wollen *to want to*

ich wollte	I wanted to	**wir wollten**	we wanted to
du wolltest	you wanted to	**ihr wolltet**	you wanted to
er wollte	he wanted to	**Sie wollten**	you wanted to
sie wollte	she wanted to	**sie wollten**	they wanted to
es wollte	it wanted to		

dürfen	to be allowed	*Imperfect*	**durfte**
können	to be able	*Imperfect*	**konnte**
müssen	to have to	*Imperfect*	**musste**
mögen	to like to	*Imperfect*	**mochte**

Please note the plural adds **-en**. The verb in the infinitive goes to the end of the sentence just as in the present tense.

49

e.g. **Er wollte einen Brief schreiben.**
He wanted to write a letter.
Ich konnte die Schrift nicht lesen.
I was not able to read the writing.
Wir durften die Strasse überqueren.
We were allowed to cross the street.
Sie mussten zu Hause bleiben.
They had to stay at home.

EXERCISE II

1 Were you able to visit her?   2 Yes, I visited her last week.
3 Did he have to go back?   4 No, he was able to stay here.
5 Was the child allowed to go out?   6 Yes, the parents allowed
it.   7 Did she want to go by car?   8 No, she wanted to go by
aeroplane.   9 Did the team win the football match?   10 Yes,
the result was 2:1.

NEW WORDS

der Autounfall	the car accident
der Fahrer	the driver
die Garage	the garage
die Schrift	the handwriting
das Flugzeug	the aeroplane
das Kind	the child
das Spiel	the play, the match
das Fussballspiel	the football match
die Mannschaft	the team
das Resultat	the result, score
sich in Verbindung setzen	to get in touch with
die Einbahnstrasse	one way street
einbiegen, bog ein (*irreg*)	to turn round a corner
austauschen	to exchange
ärgerlich sein	to be annoyed
reparieren	to repair

überqueren ✓	to cross the street
rufen, rief (*irreg*)	to call
anrufen, anrief (*irreg*)	to 'phone
schreiben, schrieb (*irreg*)	to write
zusammenstossen (*irreg*)	to collide

Lesson Nine

1 The **past participle** of **irregular verbs** ends in **-en**; as with the regular verbs it goes to the end of the sentence.

	INFINITIVE	PAST PARTICIPLE
lesen	to read	**gelesen**
sehen	to see	**gesehen**
nehmen	to take	**genommen**
essen	to eat	**gegessen**
sprechen	to speak	**gesprochen**
geben	to give	**gegeben**
helfen	to help	**geholfen**

e.g. **Haben Sie das Buch gelesen?**
Have you read the book?
Ja, ich habe es gelesen.
Yes, I have read it.
Hat sie das Paket genommen?
Did she take the parcel?
Nein, es liegt immer noch hier.
No, it is still lying here.
Haben Sie mit Ihrem Chef gesprochen?
Did you speak with your boss?
Ja, er wollte sich die Sache noch überlegen.
Yes, he wanted to think the matter over.

2 Separable verbs add **ge** after the prefix.

	INFINITIVE	PERFECT
mitnehmen	to take with	**mitgenommen**
abgeben	to hand over	**abgegeben**

52

ansehen	to look at	**angesehen**
anfangen	to begin	**angefangen**

e.g. **Er hat den Mantel mitgenommen.**
He took the coat with him.
Wir haben die Karten abgegeben.
We handed the tickets over.
Haben Sie sich die Bilder angesehen?
Did you look at the pictures?

3 There are several irregular verbs which change the vowel
and sometimes the consonant.

bringen	to bring	**gebracht**
denken	to think	**gedacht**
wissen	to know (*facts*)	**gewusst**
kennen	to know (*people, countries*)	**gekannt**
nennen	to name, to mention	**genannt**
rennen	to run	**gerannt**

e.g. **Er hat mir den Scheck gebracht.**
He has brought me the cheque.
Haben Sie seine Adresse gewusst?
Did you know his address?
Nein, ich habe sie nicht gekannt.
No, I did not know it.

4 Perfect of auxiliary verbs

The auxiliary verbs form their perfect regularly, but those
with an umlaut lose the same.

	INFINITIVE	PERFECT
müssen	to have to	**gemusst**
können	to be able to	**gekonnt**
dürfen	to be allowed to	**gedurft**
wollen	to want to	**gewollt**
but :		
mögen	to like to	**gemocht** (*irregular*)

5 However, the auxiliary verbs are much more frequently used together with another verb. In that case both verb and auxiliary are placed at the end of the sentence in the infinitive.

e.g. **Ich habe ihn begleiten wollen.**
I wanted to accompany him.
Er hat für mich bezahlen müssen.
He has had to pay for me.
Wir haben dich abholen wollen.
We wanted to fetch you.
Haben Sie im Kino rauchen dürfen?
Have you been allowed to smoke in the cinema?

EXERCISE I (Use the perfect tense.)

1 She has bought a fur coat. 2 I used to (*früher*) live in London. 3 They have shown us their shop. 4 Have you asked him? 5 Our holidays cost us a lot of money.

EXERCISE II (Use the perfect tense.)

1 Have you rented the garage? 2 No, I was not able to get one. 3 Did he drink too much? 4 No, he is quite sober. 5 Did you read my book? 6 Yes, I found it very interesting. 7 Did you have to admire him? 8 Yes, I had always to admire him. 9 Did he want to go there? 10 No, he did not want to go there.

6 Verbs which express movement or change of position form their perfect tense with **sein**—*to be*, as does **sein** itself:

Regular verbs	INFINITIVE	PERFECT TENSE
eilen	to hurry	**sie ist geeilt**
reisen	to travel	**er ist gereist**
wandern	to hike	**wir sind gewandert**
folgen	to follow	**Sie sind gefolgt**

54

Irregular verbs

	INFINITIVE	PERFECT TENSE
fahren	to drive	**ich bin gefahren**
gehen	to go	**ich bin gegangen**
wachsen	to grow	**er ist gewachsen**
kommen	to come	**sie ist gekommen**
bleiben	to stay	**wir sind geblieben**
sterben	to die	**er ist gestorben**
geschehen	to happen	**es ist geschehen**
sein	to be	**Sie sind gewesen**

e.g. **Sind Sie in die Stadt gegangen?**
Did you go to town?
Nein, ich bin zu Hause geblieben.
No, I stayed at home.
Ist sie mit dem Auto gefahren?
Did she go by car?
Ja, sie ist gerade angekommen.
Yes, she has just arrived.

EXERCISE III (Use the perfect tense).

1 Did she cross the street?   2 No, she remained on the pavement.   3 Did she hurry to the office?   4 Yes, the train was late.   5 Did the grass grow again?   6 No, it is still very yellow.

7   The pluperfect tense is formed like the perfect, but with **haben** and **sein** in the imperfect. (Just as in English we say *he had run.*) The past participle goes to the end of the clause or sentence, as it does in the perfect.

e.g. **Er hatte schon gegessen.**
He had already eaten.
Wir waren früh nach Bonn gefahren.
We had driven to Bonn early.

CONVERSATIONAL PRACTICE

Haben Sie Ihre Schuhe angezogen?	Did you put your shoes on?
Ja, ich habe sie angezogen	Yes, I have put them on.
Hat er einen Wunsch geäussert?	Did he express a wish?
Nein, er hat keinen Wunsch geäussert	No, he did not express a wish.
Bist du hungrig gewesen?	Are you hungry?
Ja, ich bin hungrig und durstig gewesen.	Yes, I am hungry and thirsty.

NEW WORDS

das Paket	the parcel	**der Bürgersteig**	the pavement
das Bild	the picture	**der Zug**	the train
die Bilder	the pictures	**der Pelzmantel**	the fur coat
die Sache	the matter	**der Laden** ⎱	the shop
der Scheck	the cheque	**das Geschäft** ⎰	
das Gras	the grass	**der Urlaub**	the holiday
aüssern	to express	**anziehen** (*irreg*)	to put on
bewundern	to admire	**finden** (*irreg*)	to find
übersetzen	to translate	**trinken** (*irreg*)	to drink
mieten	to rent	**gelb**	yellow
nüchtern	sober	**es hat Verspät-ung**	it is delayed

Lesson Ten

The **plural of nouns** is formed in various ways:

1 Masculine nouns

Monosyllabic nouns add **e** and some modify the vowel (i.e. it takes an umlaut).

	SINGULAR	PLURAL
der Zug	the train	**die Züge**
der Tag	the day	**die Tage**
der Brief	the letter	**die Briefe**
der Stuhl	the chair	**die Stühle**
der Tisch	the table	**die Tische**

Nouns which end in **e** add **n**:

der Buchstabe	the letter of the alphabet	**die Buchstaben**
der Gatte	the husband	**die Gatten**

Those ending in **el, en, er** have no additional endings, but some modify the vowel. (Note: it is always the vowel of the stressed syllable which is modified. In the case of compound nouns, the vowel of the last stressed syllable is modified.)

der Onkel	the uncle	**die Onkel**
der Vater	the father	**die Väter**
der Bruder	the brother	**die Brüder**
der Apfel	the apple	**die Äpfel**
der Fussboden	the floor	**die Fussböden**

57

2. Neuter nouns

Add **er** to short nouns and modify the vowel where possible:

das Haus	the house	**die Häuser**
das Buch	the book	**die Bücher**
das Kleid	the dress	**die Kleider**

Those ending in **er** do not change in the plural:

das Zimmer	the room	**die Zimmer**
das Fenster	the window	**die Fenster**
das Messer	the knife	**die Messer**

3 Feminine nouns

A large number of feminine nouns end in **e** and they add **n** in the plural:

die Lampe	the lamp	**die Lampen**
die Dame	the lady	**die Damen**
die Briefmarke	the stamp	**die Briefmarken**
die Tasche	the bag	**die Taschen**

Feminine nouns which end in **in** add **nen** to form the plural:

die Freundin	the girl friend	**die Freundinnen**
die Kellnerin	the waitress	**die Kellnerinnen**
die Lehrerin	the lady teacher	**die Lehrerinnen**
die Gattin	the wife	**die Gattinnen**

Exceptions to the rule are:

die Mutter	the mother	**die Mütter**
die Nacht	the night	**die Nächte**
die Holzbank	the wooden bench	**die Holzbänke**

4 **Foreign nouns** add **s** in the plural:

das Auto	the car	**die Autos**
das Kino	the cinema	**die Kinos**
das Restaurant	the restaurant	**die Restaurants**
das Hotel	the hotel	**die Hotels**
der Portier	the doorman	**die Portiers**

5 The definite articles for the plural are formed like this:

NOMINATIVE	ACCUSATIVE	DATIVE
die	**die**	**den+n**

Add **n** to form all plural nouns in the dative unless the ending is **n** already. All genders have only one plural article.

die Bücher	**die Bücher**	**den Büchern**
die Frauen	**die Frauen**	**den Frauen**
die Männer	**die Männer**	**den Männern**

6 The following adjectives are declined like the definite article **der, die, das**:

	MASCUL.	FEMIN.	NEUT.	PLURAL
	der	**die**	**das**	**die**
this	**dieser**	**diese**	**dieses**	**diese**
that	**jener**	**jene**	**jenes**	**jene**
each/every	**jeder**	**jede**	**jedes**	—
which	**welcher**	**welche**	**welches**	**welche**
many a	**mancher**	**manche**	**manches**	**manche**

e.g. **Welcher Mann kommt mir entgegen?**
Which man is coming towards me?
Welchen Mann sehen Sie?
Which man do you see?
Welche Frau gibt Ihnen das Geld?
Which woman gives you the money?
Welches Kind spielt zu Hause?
Which child plays at home?

EXERCISE I

1 Were you able to lend my friends the money? 2 Yes, I was able to lend it to them. 3 Were these houses very expensive? 4 No, they are very reasonable. 5 Are the hotels all full? 6 No, some still have a few rooms free (= vacant). 7 May we pick the apples from these trees? 8 Why not, there are plenty. 9 Have the guests gone to the cinema? 10 Unfortunately there were no more seats left.

EXERCISE II

1 Did the gentleman visit his wife? 2 Yes, but she was out. 3 Is the cheese available in England? 4 No, one cannot get it there. 5 Was this restaurant closed? 6 No, it is open every day from 10 o'clock in the morning till midnight. 7 Which hotel can you recommend? 8 I cannot recommend any. 9 Which waiter is bringing our order? 10 This waiter is just coming.

7 Some prepositions are followed by the **accusative** or the **dative** case:

an	at	**vor**	in front of
zwischen	between	**unter**	underneath
auf	on top of	**in**	in
neben	next to	**über**	above
hinter	behind		

In order to decide which case is needed the student should ask himself whether the meaning is:

wohin where to + **accusative** (*expressing movement*)
or:
wo where + **dative** (*resting position*)

60

The following list of verbs will help to distinguish the cases:

ACCUSATIVE		DATIVE	
stellen	to place	**stehen**	to stand
setzen	to set	**sitzen**	to sit
legen	to lay	**liegen**	to lie
hängen	to hang	**hängen**	to hang
	(*something*)		(*to be hanging*)
stecken	to insert	**stecken**	to pin

e.g. **Wohin stellen Sie den Teller?**
Where are you placing the plate?
Ich stelle ihn auf den Tisch.
I'm putting it on the table.
Liegt der Bleistift auch da?
Is the pencil lying there too?
Ja, er liegt auch da.
Yes, it's lying there too.
Wo hat das Bild gehangen?
Where did the picture hang?
Es hat an der Wand gehangen.
It hung on the wall.
Wohin legt er das Buch?
Where does he lay the book?
Er legt es auf den Stuhl.
He lays it on the chair.
Wo steht der Koffer?
Where does the suitcase stand?
Er steht zwischen dem Bett und dem Nachttisch.
It stands between the bed and the bedside table.
Hat er das Auto hinter das Haus gefahren?
Has he driven the car behind the house?
Nein, es steht noch vor dem Haus.
No, it is still standing in front of the house.
Was ist unter dem Fenster?
What is underneath the window?
Unter dem Fenster ist die Heizung.
The central heating is underneath the window.

61

EXERCISE III

1 Where are you going? 2 I am going to the post office. 3 What will you buy at the counter? 4 I want to buy stamps. 5 Where can you hang the calendar? 6 I can hang it on the wall. 7 Did your brother give you this present? 8 No, my sister gave it to me. 9 Did she like this dish? 10 Yes, she liked it very much and it tasted good.

NEW WORDS

leihen (*irreg*)	to lend
preiswert	reasonable (*in price*)
voll	full
erhältlich	obtainable
frei	free, vacant
mehr	more
viele	plenty, many
übrig	left over
jeden Tag	every day
empfehlen (*irreg*)	to recommend
gerade	just
schmecken	to taste
pflücken	to pick
der Baum, die Bäume	the tree(s)
der Gast, die Gäste	the guest (s)
der Platz, die Plätze	the seat (s)
der Käse, die Käse	the cheese (s)
die Bestellung, die Bestellungen	the order (s)
die Mitternacht	midnight
das Postamt, die Postämter	the post office (s)
der Schalter, die Schalter	the counter (s)
der Kalender, die Kalender	the calendar (s)
das Gericht, die Gerichte	the dish (es)

Lesson Eleven

1 As explained in Lesson Two **questions** are formed by placing the verb in front of the subject.

e.g.

POSITIVE QUESTION AND POSITIVE ANSWER

Kommen Sie heute abend?	**Ja, ich komme.**
Are you coming this evening?	Yes, I am coming.

NEGATIVE QUESTION AND NEGATIVE ANSWER

Haben Sie kein Gepäck?	**Nein, ich habe keins.**
Have you no luggage?	No, I have none.

but:

NEGATIVE QUESTION AND POSITIVE ANSWER

Haben Sie keine Kinder?	**Doch, ich habe zwei Kinder.**
Have you no children?	Oh yes, I have two children.

2 Questions referring to things rather than persons are formed by adding a preposition to **wo**.

womit	with what	**worin**	in what
wofür	for what	**woraus**	out of what

3 Expressions such as *in it, in them, under it, with it,* which are mostly replies to **womit, worin, worunter, woraus,** are formed by adding the preposition to **da**. In the case of two vowels coming together an **r** is added.

damit	with it	**darin**	in it
dafür	for it	**daraus**	out of it

e.g. **Womit schreiben Sie den Brief?**
What are you writing the letter with?
Ich schreibe ihn damit.
I am writing it with this (that).
Worin arbeiten Sie?
Where do you work?
Ich arbeite darin.
I work in there.
Worüber hängen Sie den Anzug?
What are you hanging the suit on?
Ich hänge ihn darüber.
I am hanging it on this (that).

As the examples show, the same expressions are used where in English we find a demonstrative: *this, that, those* or *these*.

4   Adjectives after nouns are treated as in English and do not change their endings.

e.g. **Das Haus ist gross.**
The house is big.
Der Sohn ist krank.
The son is ill.
Der Tisch ist rund.
The table is round.
Die Frau ist nicht dick.
The lady is not fat.

5   Adjectives before nouns must be carefully practised, as they decline.

THE USE OF ADJECTIVES AFTER A DEFINITE ARTICLE

	MASCULINE	FEMININE
Nom.	**der grüne Salat**	**die schöne Lampe**
Acc.	**den grünen Salat**	**die schöne Lampe**
Dat.	**dem grünen Salat**	**der schönen Lampe**
Gen.	**des grünen Salats**	**der schönen Lampe**

64

	NEUTER	PLURAL
Nom.	das nette Kind	die neuen Häuser
Acc.	das nette Kind	die neuen Häuser
Dat.	dem netten Kind	den neuen Häusern
Gen.	des netten Kindes	der neuen Häuser

THE USE OF ADJECTIVES AFTER AN INDEFINITE ARTICLE

	MASCULINE	FEMININE
Nom.	ein neuer Mantel	eine schöne Tasche
Acc.	einen neuen Mantel	eine schöne Tasche
Dat.	einem neuen Mantel	einer schönen Tasche
Gen.	eines neuen Mantels	einer schönen Tasche

	NEUTER	PLURAL
Nom.	ein altes Kleid	keine guten Bücher
Acc.	ein altes Kleid	keine guten Bücher
Dat.	einem alten Kleid	keinen guten Büchern
Gen.	eines alten Kleides	keiner guten Bücher

THE USE OF ADJECTIVES WITHOUT ANY ARTICLE

	MASCULINE	FEMININE
Nom.	schwarzer Kaffee	frische Butter
Acc.	schwarzen Kaffee	frische Butter
Dat.	schwarzem Kaffee	frischer Butter
Gen.	schwarzen Kaffees	frischer Butter

	NEUTER	PLURAL
Nom.	altes Brot	schlechte Eier
Acc.	altes Brot	schlechte Eier
Dat.	altem Brot	schlechten Eiern
Gen.	alten Brotes	schlechter Eier

Note that the adjective ends in **-e** in the nominative of all genders, and in the accusative of feminine and neuter genders. In the accusative masculine and in the dative and genitive of all genders, the adjective end in **-en**. After an indefinitive article the adjective must take the endings of the definite article, in order to show the case and gender of the noun that follows. The same applies when using possessive adjectives. Without an article the adjective takes the endings of the

definite article, except in the genitive case. Use of this case will be explained in a later lesson.

e.g. **Wo ist Ihr neuer Wagen?**
Where is your new car?
Er schreibt seinem kranken Sohn.
He writes to his sick son.
Die kurze Fahrt dauert nur eine halbe Stunde.
The short journey lasts only half an hour.
Heute ist der erste November.
Today is the first of November.
Am 31. Dezember ist Sylvester.
The 31st December is New Year's Eve.

EXERCISE I

1 Did your grandfather die last night?   2 Yes, he died peacefully.   3 Has the man a blind wife?   4 No, he has a deaf wife. 5 Is your clever friend very lonely?   6 No, he has many intelligent friends.

EXERCISE II (Use **wo**+preposition and answer with **da**+ preposition).

1 With what did you settle the high bill?   2 I paid by cheque. 3 From what did he drink the new wine?   4 He drank out of the old glass.   5 Out of what did you take the suit?   6 I took it out of the suitcase.

6 *What kind of* is translated in German by **was für ein?** It asks for a description or explanation. In the answer use the indefinite article. No article is used in the plural.

e.g. **Was für einen Wagen haben Sie?**
What kind of car have you got?
Ich habe einen neuen Wagen.
I have a new car.
Was für eine Bluse hat sie gekauft?
What kind of blouse did she buy?

66

Sie hat eine rote Bluse gekauft.
She has bought a red blouse.
Was für Kleider hat sie?
What kind of clothes has she got?
Sie hat moderne Kleider.
She has modern clothes.

EXERCISE III

1 What kind of a street is this? 2 This is a quiet street. 3 What kind of an office is that? 4 This is a small office. 5 What kind of a family is that? 6 This is a nice family.

CONVERSATIONAL PRACTICE

Was machen Sie?	What are you doing?
Ich schreibe an meinen klugen Freund.	I am writing to my clever friend.
Bei wem wohnt er?	With whom is he living?
Er wohnt bei seiner alten Mutter.	He is living with his old mother.
Womit schreiben Sie?	With what are you writing?
Ich schreibe mit meinem Bleistift.	I am writing with my pencil.
Ich schreibe damit.	I am writing with it.

NEW WORDS

das Brot	bread
der Salat, die Salate	the salad(s)
das Ei, die Eier	the egg(s)
die Fahrt, die Fahrten	the journey(s)
die Familie, die Familien	the family, families
der Grossvater, die Grossväter	the grandfather (s)
die Art, die Weise	the kind, the manner

67

die Schreibmaschine, die Schreibmaschinen	the typewriter (s)
der Fernschreiber	the telex
friedlich	peaceful
einsam	lonely
intelligent, klug	intelligent
stumm	dumb
taub	deaf
blind	blind
nett	nice
klein	small
taubstumm	deaf and dumb

Lesson Twelve

1 Most adjectives form their comparative regularly by adding **er** to the adjective. A number of short adjectives add an umlaut (¨) in the comparative.

ADJECTIVE		COMPARATIVE
schön	fine, beautiful	**schöner**
warm	warm	**wärmer**
süss	sweet	**süsser**
jung	young	**jünger**
alt	old	**älter**
kalt	cold	**kälter**
billig	cheap	**billiger**
teuer	expensive	**teurer**

2 The **superlative** is formed by adding **st** to the adjective. However, because the superlative cannot be used by itself (but must be preceded by a determinative word—"*the* best . . .", "*my* newest . . ." etc.) this ending has to agree with the following noun. Please note adjectives ending in **d, t, sch, z** or in a vowel, add **e** in the superlative. If the adjective is used adverbially **am** is placed before the superlative, also if comparing nouns of the same category.

SUPERLATIVE		ADVERBIALLY USED
der schönste	the finest	**am schönsten**
der wärmste	the warmest	**am wärmsten**
der süsseste	the sweetest	**am süssesten**
der jüngste	the youngest	**am jüngsten**
der älteste	the oldest	**am ältesten**
der kälteste	the coldest	**am kältesten**

69

| der billigste | the cheapest | am billigsten |
| der teuerste | the most expensive | am teuersten |

e.g. **Das ist ein schönes Zimmer.**
This is a beautiful room.
Haben Sie kein schöneres Zimmer?
Have you no nicer room?
Nein, das ist das schönste.
No, this is the nicest.
Wir suchen eine billige Wohnung.
We are looking for a cheap flat.
Wir haben eine billigere Wohnung gefunden.
We have found a cheaper flat.
Unsere Freunde haben die billigste Wohnung gemietet.
Our friends have rented the cheapest flat.

Examples of the use of nouns in the same category.

1 **Der Fluss ist tief, der See ist tiefer, aber das Meer**
The river is deep, the lake is deeper, but the ocean
ist am tiefsten.
is (the) deepest.

2 **Die Tulpe ist schön, die Nelke ist schöner, aber die**
The tulip is pretty, the carnation is prettier, but the
Rose ist am schönsten.
rose is (the) prettiest..

3 There are a number of adjectives which form their comparative and superlative irregularly.

ADJECTIVE	COMPARATIVE	SUPERLATIVE
rund round	**runder**	**am rundesten**
		der rundeste
rasch quick	**rascher**	**am raschesten**
		der rascheste
froh glad	**froher**	**am frohsten**
		der froheste
voll full	**voller**	**am vollsten**
		der vollste

COMPARATIVE		
(VERY IRREGULAR)		
gern haben	**lieber**	**am liebsten**
to like		**der liebste**
viel much	**mehr**	**am meisten**
		der meiste
oft frequently	**häufiger**	**am häufigsten**
		der häufigste
gut good	**besser**	**am besten**
		der beste
hoch high	**höher**	**am höchsten**
		der höchste
nah near	**näher**	**am nächsten**
		der nächste
bald soon	**eher**	**am ehesten**
		der eheste

EXERCISE I

1 Do you like tea or coffee? 2 I prefer coffee. 3 Was the weather colder in January or February last year? 4 It was colder in February. 5 Was the soldier more famous than the sailor? 6 The sailor was the most famous.

EXERCISE II

1 Are these papers interesting? 2 No, the books are much more interesting. 3 Is this your newest suitcase? 4 No, this is my oldest suitcase. 5 Can you show me the shortest way to the bank? 6 Yes, but the shortest way is not always the best.

The English word *than* is translated in German by **als**.

4 Infinitive Sentences

A small number of verbs govern the infinitive without **zu.**

These are:	**sehen** to see	**kommen** to come
	hören to hear	**lernen** to learn
	helfen to help	**lehren** to teach
	gehen to go	

71

e.g. **Ich hörte ihn die Treppe herauf kommen.**
I heard him coming up the stairs.
Wir halfen ihm das Essen vorbereiten.
We helped him to prepare the dinner.
Sie lehrte uns gut Deutsch sprechen.
She taught us to speak German well.
Ich lerne schwimmen.
I am learning how to swim.

but

Wir baten sie uns zu besuchen.
We asked her to visit us.
Er wünscht Karten zu spielen.
He wants to play cards.

EXERCISE III

1 Has he promised to work harder? 2 Yes, he has promised to. 3 Did you hear him coming up the stairs? 4 No, I did not hear him, he was very quiet. 5 What is there to be seen? 6 There was not much to be seen.

CONVERSATIONAL PRACTICE

Ordering a Hotel Room

Hallo, ist das der Frankfurter Hof?	Hallo, is that the Frankfurter Hof?
Kann ich bitte mit dem Empfangschef sprechen?	Can I speak to (with) reception, please?
Einen Moment bitte, ich verbinde Sie.	One moment please, I will connect you.
Ja, hier ist der Empfang, was kann ich für Sie tun?	Reception here. What can I do for you?
Ich möchte ein Einzelzimmer mit Bad.	I would like a single room with bath.
Für wann und für wie lange?	For when and for how long do you want it?

Für zwei Nächte, vom 13. bis zum 15. dieses Monats.	For two nights from the 13th to the 15th of this month.
Das geht in Ordnung. Das Zimmer kostet DM. 70.00 pro Nacht ohne Frühstück.	That seems to be all right. The room costs DM 70.00 per night without breakfast.
Danke, das passt mir gut. Ich werde so ungefähr um 12 Uhr mittags eintreffen.	Thank you, that suits me well. I shall arrive at about 12 o'clock lunch time.
Und wie ist Ihr Name?	And what is your name?
Mein Name ist Hans Müller.	My name is Hans Müller.
Gut, Herr Müller, wir erwarten Sie dann.	Very well, Mr. Müller, we shall expect you then.

NEW WORDS

From now on, in the word lists, we will show the plural form of the German nouns simply by putting in parentheses the ending or the modification to a preceding vowel. Thus, (**en**) or (**n**) shows a plural ending; (**··e**) shows the vowel modification and an ending. Should the plural form be the same as the singular, we put (–) . . . and in some cases, of course, no plural exists.

die Papiere	the papers
der Koffer (–)	the suitcase
der Weg (e)	the way
der Soldat (en)	the soldier
der Matrose (en)	the sailor
berühmt	famous
interessant	interesting
schwer arbeiten	to work hard
ruhig	quiet
es gibt	there is, there are

73

Lesson Thirteen

1 The Genitive Case

Now we are coming to the last case in German. It is used to indicate possession. Whereas in English this is shown by an apostrophe and *s*, in German the article changes.

DEFINITE ARTICLE

der—des (*m*)   **die—der** (*f*)   **das—des** (*n*)
die—der (*pl*)

INDEFINITE ARTICLE

ein—eines (*m*)   **eine—einer** (*f*)   **ein—eines** (*n*)
keine—keiner (*pl*)

Masculine and neuter nouns add **s** (or **es** in the case of monosyllabic nouns and those ending **-s, -ss, -sch, -z, -tz**, and **-ch**) to the noun in the singular. Feminine and plural nouns, however, have no separate endings.

e.g. **Ist das das Haus Ihres Freundes?**
Is that your friend's house?
Ja, das ist sein Haus.
Yes, that is his house.
Ist das die Frau dieses Mannes?
Is that this man's wife?
Nein, das ist nicht seine Frau, das ist seine Freundin.
No, that is not his wife, that is his girl friend.

74

EXERCISE I

1 Do you know this lady's brother?   2 No, I do not know him.
3 Where is your firm's office?   4 It is on the corner of the next
street.   5 Is that your brother-in-law's car?   6 No, it is not his
car, it is my sister-in-law's car.

2   Genitive Prepositions

After certain prepositions, the noun is always in the genitive
case.

statt, anstatt	instead of
diesseits	on this side of
jenseits	on that side of
ausserhalb	on the outside of
innerhalb	on the inside of
während	while, during
wegen	on account of, because of
trotz	in spite of

e.g. **Sie kommt anstatt ihres Bruders.**
She is coming instead of her brother.
Diesseits des Hauses ist der Garten.
The garden is on this side of the house.
Jenseits der Strasse ist der grosse Hauptbahnhof.
The large Central station is on that side of the street.
Er wohnt ausserhalb der Stadt.
He lives outside the town.
Ich werde Sie innerhalb einer Woche wiedersehen.
I shall see you within a week.
**Während der Vorstellung hört das Publikum
angespannt zu.**
During the performance the audience listens attentively.
Trotz der Kälte gehen wir spazieren.
In spite of the cold we are going for a walk.
**Wegen der hohen Preise können wir uns das nicht
leisten.**
On account of the high prices we cannot afford that.

75

EXERCISE II

1 Are you buying flowers for your hostess?   2 No, I am buying chocolates instead of flowers.   3 Did you meet many people during your stay in Germany?   4 Yes, I met many old friends. 5 Where is the town hall of this city?   6 You will find it in the market place.

3 Conjunctions

The following conjunctions do not change the word order (see Lesson 15, paragraph 1):

und	and
aber	but
sondern	but (*followed by a negative sentence*)
denn	for (*in the sense of 'because'*)
oder	or

These conjunctions join two main sentences which are separated by a comma, except in the case of **und** where there is no comma if the subject remains the same.

e.g. **Ich bleibe sechs Monate in Deutschland und lerne Deutsch.**
I am staying for six months in Germany and am learning German.

Er geht in das Büro, aber sie arbeitet zu Hause.
He goes to the office, but she works at home.

Die Waren sind nicht teuer, sondern sehr billig.
The goods are not expensive, but very cheap.

Wir sind sehr müde, denn wir haben sehr viel gearbeitet.
We are very tired because we have worked very hard.

Kommen Sie heute oder kommen Sie morgen?
Are you coming today or tomorrow?

76

CONVERSATIONAL PRACTICE

Ein Herr geht in das Büro von Lufthansa.
A gentleman goes into the office of Lufthansa.

Guten Morgen, kann ich Ihnen behilflich sein?
Good morning. Can I help you?

Ich möchte mit meiner Frau nach Düsseldorf fliegen.
I would like to fly to Düsseldorf with my wife.

Wann möchten Sie dorthin fliegen? Wir fliegen mehrere Male am Tage nach Düsseldorf.
When do you want to fly there? We have several flights during the day to Düsseldorf.

Wir möchten morgen früh fliegen.
We would like to go to-morrow morning.

Ich schlage Ihnen vor, das Flugzeug um 10 Uhr morgens zu nehmen. Sie kommen dann um 5 Minuten vor 11 Uhr dort an.
I suggest the ten o'clock flight, that will get you to Düsseldorf at 5 to 11.

Fliegen Sie erster oder Touristen Klasse?
Do you want to fly first or economy class?

Wir möchten erster Klasse fliegen.
We would rather fly first class.

Wann werden Sie zurückfliegen, oder bleiben Sie in Düsseldorf?
When do you want to come back, or are you staying in Düsseldorf?

Können Sie uns bitte eine Rückfahrkarte ausstellen?
Can you give us a return ticket please?

Natürlich.
Of course.

Und wann wollen Sie zurückkommen?
And when do you want to come back?

Das weiss ich noch nicht.
That I do not know yet.

Gut, ich fülle nur das Abflugsdatum aus.
Very well, I will fill in only the departure date.

77

Haben Sie Ihren Pass und den Ihrer Frau?	Have you your passport and that of your wife?
Danke schön.	Thank you.
Hier sind Ihre Flugkarten.	Here are your tickets.
Ich wünsche Ihnen eine gute Reise und ich werde die Rechnung in Ihr Büro schicken.	I wish you a good trip and shall send the bill to your office.
Auf Wiedersehen.	Good-bye.

NEW WORDS

der Schwager (—)	the brother-in-law
die Schwägerin (nen)	the sister-in-law
die Gastgeberin (nen)	the hostess
die Pralinen	the chocolates
der Aufenthalt	the stay
die Vorstellung (en)	the performance
das Publikum	the audience
das Rathaus (¨er)	the town hall
der Marktplatz (¨e)	the market-place
die Ecke (n)	the corner
die Kälte	the cold
sich leisten	to afford—*reflexive verb in German.*
die Firma (Firmen)	the company

Lesson Fourteen

1 The Interrogative Pronouns

Nom.	**wer**	who
Acc.	**wen**	whom
Dat.	**wem**	to whom
Gen.	**wessen**	✓whose

e.g. Nom. **Wer kommt nach Hause?**
   Who is coming home?

Acc. **Wen sehen Sie auf der Strasse?**
   Whom do you see on the street?

Dat. **Wem gaben Sie das Geld?**
   To whom did you give the money?

Gen. **Wessen Buch liegt auf dem Tisch?**
   Whose book is lying on the table?

OTHER INTERROGATIVE PRONOUNS

wo	where
wann	when
wie	how
wieviel	how much
wieviele	how many
wenn	whenever, if

EXERCISE I

1 Where does he live?   2 He is living in London.   3 How are you?   4 I am very well, thank you.   5 How much is this pair of shoes?   6 They cost 110 DM.   7 When is she coming next?

79

8 She will come next week.   9 Whose birthday is it to-day?
10 It is my son's birthday.

2   Weak Nouns

Add **n** or **en** in the accusative, dative and genitive singular.
Most of these nouns are masculine and add **n** or **en** in the
plural.

		SINGULAR	
e.g.	*Nom.*	**der Herr**	the gentleman
	Acc.	**den Herrn**	to the gentleman
	Dat.	**dem Herrn**	
	Gen.	**des Herrn**	of the gentleman
		PLURAL	
	Nom.	**die Herren**	the gentlemen
	Acc.	**die Herren**	the gentlemen
	Dat.	**den Herren**	to the gentlemen
	Gen.	**der Herren**	of the gentlemen

e.g. Nom. **Der Herr kommt gerade.**
The gentleman is just coming.

Acc. **Ich sehe den Herrn in seinem Büro.**
I see the gentleman in his office.

Dat. **Wir helfen dem alten Herrn über die Strasse.**
We are helping the old man to cross the street.

Gen. **Das Geld des Herrn liegt auf dem Tisch.**
The gentleman's money is lying on the table.

OTHER WEAK NOUNS

der Mensch	the human being
der Konkurrent	the business rival
der Junge	the boy
der Knabe	the boy
der Polizist	the policeman
der Schmerz	the pain
der Name	the name
der Buchstabe	the letter of the alphabet
der Kollege	the colleague
der Gatte	the husband

80

der **Tourist**	the tourist
der **Gedanke** (des Gedankens, *Gen.*)	the thought
der **Kunde**	the customer, client
der **Glaube** (des Glaubens, *Gen.*)	the belief
der **Nachbar** (des Nachbars, *Gen.*)	the neighbour
der **Bekannte**	the acquaintance
der **Verwandte**	the relation
der **Beamte**	the official

EXERCISE II

1 Are you writing to Mr. Smith? 2 Yes, I am writing to him. 3 Will you invite your colleague? 4 No, I do not want to invite him. 5 Where is his neighbour's dog? 6 He has run away. 7 What is the name of your aquaintance? 8 I am sorry, but I do not know his name.

3 Nouns which are formed from verbs are also considered "weak nouns"; if preceded by an indefinite article they must show either a masculine or feminine ending.

der **Angestellte** the employee	ein **Angestellter**	eine **Angestellte**
der **Vorsitzende** the chairman	ein **Vorsitzender**	eine **Vorsitzende**
der **Reisende** the traveller	ein **Reisender**	eine **Reisende**
der **Erwachsene** the adult	ein **Erwachsener**	eine **Erwachsene**
der **Abgeordnete** the Member of Parliament	ein **Abgeordneter**	eine **Abgeordnete**

e.g. **Er ist ein Angestellter der Firma.**
He is an employee of the Company.
Ich kenne den Reisenden gut.
I know the traveller well.
Sie ist eine bekannte Abgeordnete.
She is a well known M.P.

4 Ordinal Numbers

der, die erste	the 1st
der, die zweite	the 2nd
der, die dritte	the 3rd
der, die vierte	the 4th
der, die fünfte	the 5th
der, die sechste	the 6th
der, die siebte	the 7th
der, die achte	the 8th
der, die neunte	the 9th
der, die zehnte	the 10th
der, die elfte	the 11th
der, die zwölfte	the 12th
der, die dreizehnte	the 13th
der, die vierzehnte	the 14th
der, die fünfzehnte	the 15th
der, die sechzehnte	the 16th
der, die siebzehnte	the 17th
der, die achtzehnte	the 18th
der, die neunzehnte	the 19th
der, die zwanzigste	the 20th

From the 20th the ordinal numbers add **-ste**; they also decline like adjectives before a noun.

e.g. **London, den achtundzwanzigsten Dezember neunzehnhundert sechsundsiebzig.**
London, the 28th December 1976.

but:

Heute ist der achtundzwanzigste Dezember.
Today is the 28th December.

EXERCISE III

1 Is the employee's job well paid? 2 Yes, it is very well paid.
3 Is the waiting-room only for travellers? 4 No, everybody
can use it. 5 With whom were you talking? 6 I was talking
with the official. 7 What date it is to-day? 8 To-day is the
20th December 1978.

NEW WORDS

das Paar (e)	the pair
ein paar Minuten	a few minutes
der Geburtstag (e)	the birthday
nächste Woche	next week
der Hund (e)	the dog
die Stellung (en)	the job
der Wartesaal (-säle)	the waiting-room
schreiben an (+*accusative*)	to write to
einladen (+*dative*)	to invite
jedermann	everybody
alle	all

Lesson Fifteen

1 Word Order. When a subordinate clause begins with a conjunction, the verb is placed at the end of the clause. The most important subordinate conjunctions are:

dass	that	**bevor**	before
ob	whether	**da**	as
weil	because	**als**	when (*mainly used*
wenn	if, whenever		*if the action is past*)
obgleich	although	**nachdem**	after

In the case of separable verbs the verb goes to the end of the sentence or clause and does not separate. If the subordinate clause precedes the main clause the verb is placed at the end of the clause, the verb and the subject of the main clause must then be inverted; thus two verbs or auxiliary and verb come together separated by a comma.

MAIN CLAUSE AT THE BEGINNING

e.g. **Er hat geschrieben, dass er heute abend kommt.**
He wrote that he is coming this evening.
Ich fahre nach Amerika, wenn ich Geld habe.
I am going to America if I have the money.
Sie bleibt heute zu Hause, weil sie viel Arbeit hat.
She is staying at home because she has a lot of work.

SUBORDINATE CLAUSE AT THE BEGINNING

Als wir gestern in der Stadt waren, machten wir einige Besorgungen.
When we were in town yesterday, we did some shopping.

Nachdem ich aufgewacht bin, ging ich ins Badezimmer.
After I woke up, I went to the bathroom.
Da das Wetter so schlecht war, gingen sie ins Kino.
As the weather was so bad, they went to the cinema.

EXERCISE I

1 Where can I get a ticket?   2 If you want to buy a ticket you must go to the ticket office.   3 Is he not coming because it is snowing?   4 Oh, yes he is coming, although it is snowing.   5 Where do you stay in London?   6 The last time I was in London I stayed with friends.

2   The Adverb

In German nearly all adjectives used as adverbs remain unchanged, and do not decline.

e.g. **Die Menschen sind nicht immer gut.**
People are not always good.
Der Student lernt gut.
The student learns well.

ADVERBS OF TIME

bald	soon	**immer**	always
dann	then	**jetzt**	now
gleich	at once	**oft**	often
schon	already		

ADVERBS OF MANNER

besonders	specially	**ungefähr**	about
genug	enough	**vielleicht**	perhaps
sehr	very	**wahrscheinlich**	probably

ADVERBS OF PLACE

dort	there	**aussen, draussen**	out (side)
hier	here	**innen, drinnen**	in (side)

85

e.g. **Wir bekommen jetzt ein Telefon.**
We are now getting a telephone.
Wenn Sie gleich mitgehen, können wir das noch erledigen.
If you come with us at once, we can still settle it.
Sie hat den Brief schon geschrieben.
She has already written the letter.
Haben Sie genug gegessen?
Have you eaten enough?
Vielleicht ist es noch möglich Karten für das Theater zu bekommen.
Perhaps it is still possible to get tickets for the theatre.

3 Order of adverbs

When there is more than one adverb, the order to follow is:
time—manner—place

e.g. **Er kommt jeden Tag zu uns.**
He comes to our house (us) every day.
Wir fahren immer schnell.
We always drive quickly.
Sie lebten wahrscheinlich in dieser Stadt.
They probably lived in this town.

EXERCISE II

1 Do you know when the bus arrives?   2 No, I do not know
the exact time.   3 Has your partner been ill?   4 No, but
every time I wanted to speak to him he was not there.   5 Can
you tell me when the ship docks in Southampton?   6 When
we docked there the last time we had to wait a long time for
the customs official.

4   Nicht always comes *before* a preposition, the past participle,
the infinitive, an adjective or an adverb. It comes *after* the
object (unless preceded by an adjective), and *at the end* of a
sentence, especially in the imperative.

86

e.g. **Bitte stellen Sie den Tisch nicht vor den Stuhl.**
Please do not place the table in front of the chair.
Er ist nicht ausgegangen.
He did not go out.
Wir haben nicht genügend Geld.
We have not enough money.
**Sie haben beschlossen das Fernsehprogramm nicht
   zu sehen.**
They have decided not to watch the television programme.
Sie kauft das blaue Kleid nicht.
She does not buy the blue dress.
Kommen Sie morgen nicht!
Do not come tomorrow.

CONVERSATIONAL PRACTICE

Fahren Sie lieber mit dem Schiff oder mit dem Flugzeug?
Do you prefer to travel by boat or by aeroplane?

Ich fahre lieber mit dem Schiff, weil ich dann mehr von der Welt sehen kann.
I prefer to go by ship, because I can then see more of the world that way.

Wo wird das Boot anlegen?
Where will the ship dock?

Es fährt zuerst nach Hamburg, dann an der Küste entlang nach Antwerpen.
It sails first to Hamburg then along the coast to Antwerp.

Von da geht es durch den Kanal in den Atlantischen Ozean und es kommt zuletzt nach New York.
From there through the Channel into the Atlantic Ocean, and it will finally dock in New York.

NEW WORDS

die Besorgungen machen	to go shopping
der Fahrkartenschalter (-)	the ticket office
der Bus (se)	the bus
der Teilhaber (-)	the partner (business)
krank	ill
anlegen	to berth, to dock
lieber haben	to prefer
die Küste (n)	the coast
der Zollbeamte (n)	the customs official
der Kanal (¨e)	the Channel
der Atlantische Ozean	the Atlantic Ocean
zuletzt	finally

Lesson Sixteen

1 Relative Pronouns

The relative pronouns are the same as the definite article, except in the genitive and in the dative plural.

	MASC.	FEM.	NEUT.	PLUR.
Nom.	**der**	**die**	**das**	**die**
Acc.	**den**	**die**	**das**	**die**
Dat.	**dem**	**der**	**dem**	**denen**
Gen.	**dessen**	**deren**	**dessen**	**deren**

2 Please note that the word order is affected. The verb goes to the end of the relative clause, as is the case with the sub-ordinate conjunctions in Lesson Fifteen.

The pronouns **welcher, welche, welches, welche**, are sometimes used, especially when referring to things. However, there is no genitive case for these pronouns.

e.g. **Ist das das Buch, das Sie lesen?**
Is that the book which you are reading?
Das ist der Brief, den ich gesucht habe.
That is the letter which I have been looking for.

3 If a preposition precedes the relative pronoun, the latter must be in the case required after the preposition.

e.g. **Die Frau, mit der Sie sprechen, ist meine Mutter.**
The lady with whom you are speaking is my mother.
Die Leute, bei denen Sie eingeladen waren, sind meine Freunde.
The people by whom you were invited are friends of mine.

Das Kino, in dem ich den guten Film gesehen habe, ist in der Mitte der Stadt.
The cinema where I saw the excellent film is in the town centre.

The relative clause in German is always preceded by a comma.

4 When referring to inanimate objects or things one can use **was, wo**, or **wo**+Preposition.

e.g. **Er fragt, wo man am besten isst.**
He asks where one can eat best.
Sie wollte wissen, was mir in diesem Land am besten gefällt.
She wanted to know what I liked best in this country.
Der Stoff, woraus das Kleid besteht, ist Baumwolle.
The material out of which the dress is made is cotton.

EXERCISE I

1 Where is the typewriter on which you want to type this letter?   2 It is standing right in front of you.   3 Is that the hotel in which you have reserved a room for us?   4 No, it is the one on the other side of the street.   5 Is that the newspaper article about which you have spoken?   6 Yes, that is the article which I found very interesting.   7 Are these the sausages whose skins are so tough?   8 No, they are not the same.

EXERCISE II

1 He gave me a cassette recorder which was very expensive. 2 How do you like the furniture which I bought in the sale? 3 I made a new dish which everybody enjoyed.   4 The new attaché case, in which he carries his papers, was very full.   5 Can you recommend a book from which I can learn?   6 Whatever he said made no sense.

CONVERSATIONAL PRACTICE

das Wetter	the weather
Wie ist das Wetter?	What is the weather like?
Es ist heute kalt.	It is cold to-day.
Hat es heute morgen geschneit?	Did it snow this morning?
Nein, es hat viel geregnet.	No, it rained a lot.
War es gestern neblig?	Was it foggy yesterday?
Nein, die Sonne hat geschienen.	No, the sun was shining.
Es friert.	It is freezing.
Ich ziehe meine wärmsten Sachen an.	I am putting my warmest things on.
Es hat die ganze Nacht gefroren.	It was freezing all night.
Wir hatten gestern sehr schönes Wetter.	We had very fine weather yesterday.
Es ist heute sehr schön.	It's a fine day today.
Glauben Sie, dass es später regnen wird?	Do you think it will rain later?
Nein, es ist viel zu windig.	No, it is much too windy.
Sie vergessen, dass wir Südwind haben.	You forget that the wind is in the south.
Macht nichts; heute regnet es nicht.	That doesn't matter; it won't rain today.
Es war gestern schrecklich heiss und schwül.	It was dreadfully hot and close yesterday.
Es kann sein, dass wir ein Gewitter bekommen, aber danach wird es sich wieder aufklären.	We may get a storm, but it will clear up again later on.
Ich nehme das Wetter, wie es kommt.	I take the weather as it comes.
Ich habe gern frische Luft.	I am very fond of fresh air.
Ich gehe nicht viel aus.	I don't go out much.
Wir gehen jeden Tag spazieren.	We go for a walk every day.

91

NEW WORDS

der Kassettenrekorder (-)	the cassette recorder
das Tonbandgerät (**e**)	the tape recorder
die andere Seite	the other side
der Artikel (-)	the article
die Wurst (**¨e**)	the sausage
die Haut (**¨e**)	the skin
das Möbel (-)	the piece of furniture
der Ausverkauf	the sale
die Aktentasche (**n**)	the attaché case
das Dokument (**e**)	the business paper, document
reservieren	to reserve
zäh	tough
sinnlos	no sense, senseless
die Sonne	the sun
der Mond	the moon
der Stern (**e**)	the star
der Regen, regnen,	the rain, to rain
der Schnee, schneien	the snow, to snow
der Hagel, hageln	the hail, to hail
der Donner, donnern	the thunder, to thunder
der Blitz, blitzen	the lightning, to flash

92

Lesson Seventeen

We have already mentioned the *familiar* forms **du** and **ihr** in Lesson One, Lesson Six and Lesson Eight; **du** is used in the Singular and **ihr** in the Plural when addressing members of one's family, close friends, children and animals.

1 **Du** and **ihr** used with **regular** verbs:

	Singular	*Plural*	
Present	**du machst**	**ihr macht**	you make
	du liebst	**ihr liebt**	you love
Imperfect	**du machtest**	**ihr machtet**	you made
	du liebtest	**ihr liebtet**	you loved
Perfect	**du hast gemacht**	**ihr habt gemacht**	you have made
	du hast geliebt	**ihr habt geliebt**	you have loved

2 **Du** and **ihr** used with **irregular** verbs:

Present	**du gibst**	**ihr gebt**	you give
	du liest	**ihr lest**	you read
Imperfect	**du gabst**	**ihr gabt**	you gave
	du last	**ihr last**	you read
Perfect	**du hast gegeben**	**ihr habt gegeben**	you have given
	du hast gelesen	**ihr habt gelesen**	you have read

3 The cases and possessive forms of **du** and **ihr** are as follows:

	Nom.	Acc.	Dat.	Possessive
du—you(*s*)	**du**	**dich**	**dir**	**dein**
ihr—you(*pl*)	**ihr**	**euch**	**euch**	**euer**

e.g. **Was willst du essen?**
What do you want to eat?
Wo wart ihr gestern?
Where were you last night?
Ich habe dich am Montag nicht in der Vorlesung gesehen.
I did not see you on Monday in the lecture.
Könnt ihr morgen abend zu uns kommen?
Can you come to our house to-morrow evening?
Wo ist der Brief, den er euch gegeben hat?
Where is the letter which he gave to you?

4 When **du** and **ihr** are used in the present tense of the **auxiliary verbs**, the familiar forms are:

to have	**du hast**	**ihr habt**
to be	**du bist**	**ihr seid**
must, to have to	**du musst**	**ihr müsst**
can, to be able to	**du kannst**	**ihr könnt**
may, to be allowed to	**du darfst**	**ihr dürft**
will, to want to	**du willst**	**ihr wollt**
to like to	**du magst**	**ihr mögt**

5 The imperfect tense of these auxiliary verbs has **du** and **ihr** forms as follows:

to have	**du hattest**	**ihr hattet**
to be	**du warst**	**ihr wart**
must, to have to	**du musstest**	**ihr musstet**
can, to be able to	**du konntest**	**ihr konntet**
may, to be allowed to	**du durftest**	**ihr durftet**
will, to want to	**du wolltest**	**ihr wolltet**
to like to	**du mochtest**	**ihr mochtet**

94

EXERCISE I (Use **du** and **ihr**)

1 What kind of programme did you see last night on T.V.?
2 We saw our favourite programme.   3 Did you have a nice
holiday last summer?   4 No, it was much too hot.   5 Are
you expecting your best friend next spring?   6 Yes, I am expecting her.

EXERCISE II (Use **du** and **ihr**)

1 Shall we give you a cheque for the transaction?   2 Yes,
thank you, I am a bit short of cash.   3 What are you doing
next Sunday?   4 We shall come to your house for tea.   5 I
would like to thank you for your kindness.   6 Do not mention
it, it was a pleasure.

6   Countries and Nationalities

The neuter article is used for almost every country except:

die Schweiz	Switzerland
die Türkei	Turkey
die Tschechoslowakei	Czechoslovakia
die Niederlande	the Netherlands
die Vereinigten Staaten	United States

e.g. **das England**—England
    der Engländer (*m*)   **die Engländerin** (*f*)
das Italien—Italy
    der Italiener (*m*)   **die Italienerin** (*f*)
das Deutschland—Germany
    der Deutsche(*m*)(*weak*) **die Deutsche** (*f*)
das Frankreich—France
    der Franzose(*m*)(*weak*) **die Französin** (*f*)
das Russland—Russia
    der Russe (*m*)   **die Russin** (*f*)
das Amerika—America
    der Amerikaner (*m*)   **die Amerikanerin** (*f*)
die Schweiz—Switzerland
    der Schweizer(*m*)   **die Schweizerin** (*f*)

95

NEW WORDS

Das Programm (e)	the programme
der Scheck (s)	the cheque
die Transaktion (en)	the transaction
das Lieblingsprogramm	the favourite programme
knapp bei Kasse	short of cash
zum Tee/Kaffee	for tea/coffee
erwarten	to expect
es ist gern geschehen	do not mention it
das Vergnügen	the pleasure
nichts zu danken	it was a pleasure

Lesson Eighteen

1 As already shown in Lesson Five when we discussed the perfect tense, **separable verbs** have to separate when the stress is on the first syllable, However, they do not separate when sent to the end of the clause or the sentence, especially after the auxiliaries and those conjunctions which change the word order.

e.g. **ausgehen**   to go out
     zurückkommen   to come back
     anfangen   to begin
     aufmachen   to open

  Er geht heute abend nicht aus.
  He is not going out this evening.
  Wann kommen Sie zurück?
  When are you coming back?

but:

  Sie wollte nicht mit der Hausarbeit anfangen.
  She did not want to start with the housework.
  Als ich die Tür aufmachte, sah ich den Briefträger
    die Strasse herunterkommen.
  When I opened the door, I saw the postman coming down the street.

2 If the verb is reflexive as well as separable the reflexive pronoun stays with the Verb. In a question or after an auxiliary, the reflexive pronoun follows the personal pronoun.

                      with accusative
e.g. **sich anziehen**   to dress oneself
     sich ausziehen   to undress oneself
     sich umziehen   to change one's clothes

97

Morgens ziehe ich mich schnell an.
In the morning I dress quickly.
Abends zieht er sich nicht immer gern aus.
In the evening he does not always like to undress.

		with dative
e.g.	**sich einbilden**	to have a high opinion of oneself
	sich vornehmen	to plan
	sich ansehen	to look at

Present tense	**Warum bildest du dir so viel ein?**
	Why are you so conceited?
Imperfect	**Welches Schloss sahst du dir gestern an?**
	Which castle did you look at yesterday?
Perfect tense	**Was haben Sie sich für morgen vorgenommen?**
	What have you planned for to-morrow?

EXERCISE I

1 Did you post the letter? 2 Yes, I posted it. 3 How does one use the telephone in the telephone booth? 4 You must insert 20 Pfennig. 5 When did he get up yesterday? 6 He got up at noon.

EXERCISE II

1 Were you surprised when he forwarded the letter to you? 2 No, I expected it. 3 Can the child dress himself already? 4 Yes, he can do it himself. 5 Have you been to the new exhibition? 6 No, but I want to see it.

3 Lassen is another auxilary verb. It is very irregular, as the examples will show. It implies that you allow a person to do something, or that you must pay for it in money or in kind.

e.g. Present **Die Eltern lassen ihr Kind ins Kino gehen.**
The parents let their child go to the cinema.

Imperfect	**Wir liessen den Mann das Gepäck tragen.**
	We had the man carry the luggage.
Perfect	**Haben Sie den Wagen von der Garage**
	reparieren lassen?
	Have you had the car repaired at the garage?

Lassen can also be used reflexively and it is followed by either the accusative case or the dative case.

e.g. **Der Gast lässt sich rasieren.**
The guest is having a shave.
Er liess dir ein Kleid machen
He had a dress made for you.
Ich habe mir das Haar legen lassen.
I have had my hair set.
Wir haben uns ein neues Haus bauen lassen.
We have had a new house built.

The third possibility of using **lassen** is reflexive and impersonal. The English language expresses it by: *can be done.*

e.g. **Es lässt sich erklären.**
It can be explained.
Der Lärm lässt sich nicht ertragen.
The noise cannot be endured.
Der Kuchen lässt sich essen.
The cake is edible.

EXERCISE III

1 Let me add greetings to your letter. 2 Why not? Here it is.
3 Can I have a cup of coffee please?   4 Very well, I will have
a pot of coffee sent to your room.   5 Have you had the letter
translated?   6 Yes, but they found it very difficult.

4 Letters

In a letter addressed to a company, if the recipient is unknown the salutation is:

Sehr geehrte Herren,
Dear Sirs,

However, in a letter to an authority no salutation is necessary. If the name of the recipient is known the salutation is then:

Sehr geehrter Herr Müller,
Dear Mr. Miller,

In the case of a married lady:

Sehr geehrte Frau Maier,
Dear Mrs. Maier,

and in the case of an unmarried lady:

Sehr geehrtes Fräulein Schmitt,
Dear Miss Smith,

If the recipient has a title it must be mentioned in the salutation;

Sehr geehrter Herr Dr. Braun,
Dear Dr. Brown,

A formal letter is concluded with:

Hochachtungsvoll (*or* **Hochachtend**)
Yours faithfully,

A little less formal:

Mit freundlichen Grüssen,
With kind regards,

To start a personal letter one says:

Lieber Hans, or **Liebe Maria,**
Dear Hans, Dear Mary,

A personal letter is concluded by a suitable phrase *e.g.*

mit vielen lieben Grüssen,
with many kind regards,

NEW WORDS

die Ausstellung (en)	the exhibition
die Telefonzelle (n)	the telephone -booth
der Mittag	the noon
der Gruss (die Grüsse)	the greeting
die Kanne (n)	the pot
das Kännchen	the little pot (*especially used in a café.*)
einwerfen (*irreg*)	to insert, to post
abnehmen (*irreg*)	to lift off
aufgeben (*irreg*)	to hand in
aufstehen (*irreg*)	to get up
nachschicken	to forward (*a letter*)
sich wundern	to be surprised
sich ansehen (*irreg*)	to look at
tun (*irreg*)	to do

Lesson Nineteen

The auxiliary verb **werden** can be used in several ways.

1 to become (with future sense of 'is going to be')
2 future tense
3 the passive voice

1 werden—*to become*

ich werde	I become	**wir werden**	we become
du wirst	you become	**ihr werdet**	you become
er wird	he becomes	**Sie werden**	you become
sie wird	she becomes	**sie werden**	they become
es wird	it becomes		

e.g. **Ich werde Lehrerin.**
I am going to be a teacher.
Er wird krank.
He is becoming ill.
Sie werden Kaufmann.
You are going to be a business man.

When a profession is referred to the indefinite article is omitted.

2 The future tense is expressed with the auxiliary verb **werden** and the infinitive of the verb. The infinitive goes to the end of the clause or the sentence as is the case when using all other auxiliaries. In German the future with **werden** is used if there is an intention to do something in the future. If

102

a specific time is mentioned, then the simple present tense may be used, as in English.

e.g. **Es wird nicht regnen.**
It will not rain.
Es wird morgen wohl schneien.
It will probably snow to-morrow.
Ich werde nächste Woche nach Berlin fliegen.
I shall fly to Berlin next week.
Ich fliege nächste Woche nach Berlin.
I am flying to Berlin next week.

3 The passive voice

The passive voice in German is formed with **werden** and the past participle. German uses the passive voice when something is done to the subject of the sentence.

To change a sentence from the active voice to the passive voice, the object of the active sentence becomes the subject of the passive sentence. The English word *by* is translated by **von** in German. If the subject in the active voice is **man** (*one*), it is omitted in the passive voice.

PRESENT TENSE

ich werde geschimpft	I am being scolded
du wirst gefragt	you are asked
er wird gesehen	he is seen
sie wird gefunden	she is found
es wird gegessen	it is being eaten
wir werden geschimpft	we are being scolded
ihr werdet gefragt	you are asked
Sie werden gesehen	you are seen
sie werden gefunden	they are found

e.g. Active: **Meine Mutter küsst mich.**
My mother kisses me.
Passive: **Ich werde von meiner Mutter geküsst.**
I am kissed by my mother.

103

The Imperfect of **werden** is **wurde.**

ich wurde gefragt	I was asked
du wurdest geschimpft	you were (being) scolded
er wurde gesehen	he was seen
sie wurde gefunden	she was found
es wurde gegessen	it was (being) eaten
wir wurden geschimpft	we were (being) scolded
ihr wurdet gefragt	you were asked
Sie wurden gesehen	you were seen
sie wurden gefunden	they were found

e.g. Active : **Meine Mutter küsste mich.**
My mother kissed me.

Passive : **Ich wurde von meiner Mutter geküsst.**
I was kissed by my mother.

The perfect tense of the passive voice is formed with **sein-** *to be.* The participle form of **werden** in the passive voice has no **ge-** if it is used together with another verb.

PERFECT TENSE

ich bin gefragt worden	I have been asked
du bist gesehen worden	you have been seen
er ist geschimpft worden	he has been scolded
sie ist gefunden worden	she has been found
es ist gegessen worden	it has been eaten
wir sind geschimpft worden	we have been scolded
ihr seid gefragt worden	you have been asked
Sie sind gesehen worden	you have been seen
sie sind gefunden worden	they have been found

e.g. Active : **Meine Mutter hat mich geküsst.**
My mother has kissed me.

Passive : **Ich bin von meiner Mutter geküsst worden.**
I have been kissed by my mother.

ich werde gefragt werden	I shall be asked
du wirst gesehen werden	you will be seen
er wird geschimpft werden	he will be scolded
sie wird gefunden werden	she will be found
es wird gegessen werden	it will be eaten
wir werden geschimpft werden	we will be scolded
ihr werdet gefragt werden	you will be asked
Sie werden gesehen werden	you will be seen
sie werden gefunden werden	they will be found

e.g. Active : **Meine Freundin wird mich küssen.**
My girlfriend will kiss me.

Passive : **Ich werde von meiner Freundin geküsst werden.**
I shall be kissed by my girlfriend.

EXERCISE I

1 Will it rain to-morrow?   2 No, I do not think so.   3 Is he studying in Germany?   4 No, but he will be studying there. 5 Has she become rich?   6 Yes, an old aunt left her a lot of money.

EXERCISE II

1 Was the man injured in the accident?   2 Yes, he has just been operated on.   3 Is the concert being broadcast on the radio?   4 Yes, you can hear it this evening.   5 Where is the newspaper printed?   6 It will be printed in London.

4 If an auxiliary verb is included in a passive sentence then the auxiliary verb is conjugated.

e.g. Present tense : **Die Schuhe müssen geputzt werden.**
The shoes have to be cleaned.

Imperfect : **Das Kleid konnte gereinigt werden.**
The dress could be cleaned.

105

Perfect tense: **Die Speisekarte hat gedruckt werden müssen.**
The menu-card had to be printed.

Future tense: **Die Frau wird operiert werden müssen.**
The lady will have to be operated on.

5 In a subordinate clause the auxiliary verb goes to the end of the clause.

e.g. **Er fuhr den Wagen, der von seinem Freund repariert werden musste.**
He drove the car which had to be repaired by his friend.
Wir besuchen unsere Freundin, wenn sie ins Krankenhaus eingeliefert werden muss.
We will visit our friend if she has to be admitted into hospital.

EXERCISE III

1 Can you come for dinner at eight o'clock?   2 If I am told in time I will be able to come at 8 o'clock.   3 When is the book being published?   4 If the author can be persuaded, it will appear in the summer.   5 By whom will he be examined?
6 The doctor, who may be called at short notice, will be able to examine him.

NEW WORDS

der Unfall (¨e)	the accident
der Schriftsteller (-)	the author
zur Zeit, rechtzeitig	in time
heute abend	this evening
studieren	to study
hinterlassen (*irreg*)	to bequeath
operieren	to operate
übertragen (*irreg*)	to broadcast, to transfer
drucken	to print
verlegen	to publish

überreden	to persuade
untersuchen	to examine
erscheinen (*irreg*)	to appear
einliefern	to admit (to hospital)
in Kürze	at short notice

Lesson Twenty

1 There are a number of verbs which govern a direct object in English but which in German necessitate the use of an indirect object. Some of the most commonly used verbs in this category are:

sagen	to say	**helfen**	to help
erzählen	to tell, to relate	**verbieten**	to forbid
mitteilen	to inform	**gehorchen**	to obey
geben	to give	**befehlen**	to command
		folgen	to follow

These verbs, when used in the passive, are usually introduced by the impersonal pronoun **es**.

e.g. **Es wird mir gesagt, dass er auf mich wartet.**
I am told that he is waiting for me.

The pronoun **es** may be omitted in the impersonal passive voice. In that case the dative pronoun and the verb are inverted.

e.g. **Uns wird erzählt, dass Sie heute abend kommen wollen.**
We are told that you want to come this evening.
Ihnen ist mitgeteilt worden, dass die Ware fertig ist.
You have been informed that the goods are ready.

2 Although the passive is used much more in German than in English and particularly in the written language, the Germans prefer to use the active voice with **man**, with its simpler construction.

e.g. **Man folgte mir in die Schule.**
I was followed to school.
Man verbietet ihm, den Rasen zu betreten.
He was forbidden to step onto the grass.
Man hat ihr befohlen, eine Fremdsprache zu lernen.
She has been ordered to learn a foreign language.

EXERCISE I

1 Were you followed to the station? 2 No, I did not notice anything in particular. 3 What were you ordered to do in that case? 4 I was told to report it to the police. 5 Was he forbidden to smoke? 6 Yes, I think so, but he decided to smoke less.

EXERCISE II

1 Was she informed of the arrival of the aeroplane? 2 Yes, she has been informed. 3 Was he told that the tax has been increased? 4 No, he had no idea about it. 5 Was it very rough when you crossed the lake? 6 No, the lake was very calm. 7 Do the banks close on Saturdays? 8 Yes, they are closed.

3 Some nouns have different meanings denoted by different genders. The plural varies with some words.

der Kiefer (–)	the jaw
die Kiefer (–)	the fir tree
der Leiter (–)	the leader
die Leiter (–)	the step-ladder
die Steuer (n)	the tax
das Steuer (–)	the steering wheel
die Bank (en)	the bank
die Bank (¨e)	the bench
das Wort (e)	the written text
das Wort (¨er)	the individual word

109

der See (n)	the lake
die See (–)	the ocean, the sea
der Messer (–)	the measure
das Messer (–)	the knife
der Band (¨e)	the volume
das Band (¨er)	the tape, the ribbon

e.g. **Wir gehen auf die Bank um Geld abzuheben.**
We are going to the bank to draw out some money.
Er sass auf der Bank und ruhte sich aus.
He sat on the bench and had a rest.
Die Worte in diesem Abschnitt sind auf Englisch.
The words in this paragraph are in English.
Schlagen Sie diese Wörter im Wörterbuch nach.
Look up these words in the dictionary.

CONVERSATIONAL PRACTICE

An der Theaterkasse.	At the ticket-office in a theatre.
Eine Dame geht an die Vorverkaufskasse im Theater.	A lady goes to the advance booking office in the theatre.
Werden hier Karten für heute abend verkauft?	Can I get tickets here for this evening?
Wo möchten Sie sitzen?	Where would you like to sit?
Ich sitze am liebsten im ersten Parkett.	I prefer to sit in the front stalls.
Es tut mir leid, aber wir haben nur noch Karten für den ersten Rang.	I am very sorry but we only have tickets for the front of the dress circle left.
Gut, ich werde sie nehmen, obwohl sie teurer sind als ich bezahlen wollte.	Very well, I shall take them, although they are more than I wanted to pay.
Wann beginnt die Vorstellung?	When does the performance begin?
Um halb neun Uhr (20.30).	At half past eight.

Beim Eintritt in den Zuschauerraum.	On entering the auditorium.
Bitte beachten Sie das Schild:	Please observe the notice:
Hier wird nicht geraucht.	Smoking is forbidden here.
Möchten Sie ein Programm?	Would you like a programme?
Ja, bitte.	Yes, please.
Was kostet es?	How much is it?
50 Pfennig, bitte.	50 Pfennig, please.
Jetzt beginnt das Schauspiel, und der Vorhang geht auf.	The play begins and the curtain rises.

NEW WORDS

die Ware (n)	the goods
die Polizei	the police
die Ankunft	the arrival
abheben (*irreg*)	to draw money from the bank
sich ausruhen	to rest
nachschlagen (*irreg*)	to look up a word
bemerken	to notice
melden	to report
verbieten (*irreg*)	to forbid
mitteilen	to inform
erhöhen, steigern	to increase
stürmisch	stormy
beschliessen (*irreg*)	to decide
windstill	calm
der Abschnitt (e)	paragraph

Lesson Twenty-One

1 The prefixes **hin-** and **her-** are used with verbs of movement where **her-** expresses movement towards and **hin-** movement away from the speaker.

e.g. **Er geht in das Zimmer hinein.**
He goes into the room.

Er kommt aus dem Kino heraus.
He comes out of the cinema.

Kommen Sie die Treppe herauf!
Come up the stairs.

Gehen Sie in den Keller hinunter.
Go down to the cellar.

One often combines these words with **da** or **dort** as it is essential to give the direction in German. In forming a question concerning direction, **wo-** is prefixed to **hin** and **her**.

e.g. **Wohin gehen Sie?**
Where are you going to?

Ich gehe dorthin.
I am going there.

Woher kommt er?
Where does he come from?

Er kommt von dorther.
He is coming from there.

112

2 The **comparative** and **superlative** of adjectives are placed in front of nouns. When these adjectives are placed in front of the noun they must have the appropriate endings (the same as shown in Lesson Twelve).

e.g. **Er hat einen jüngeren Bruder als ich.**
He has a younger brother than I have.
Sie hat eine ältere Schwester.
She has an older sister.
Sie haben die kleinste Wohnung von uns allen.
You have the smallest flat of all of us.
Wir haben dem jüngsten Jungen in der Klasse ein Märchenbuch gegeben.
We have given the youngest boy in the class a story book.
Das Zimmer des ältesten Sohnes liegt in der Mansarde.
The room of the oldest son is in the attic.
Die Schlüssel der jüngsten Tochter sind verloren gegangen.
The keys of the youngest daughter are missing.

EXERCISE I

1 Can you tell me who serves the best cup of coffee here?   2 The Schloss Café serves the best coffee here.   3 What is the weather like in England in summer?   4 It is hottest in July and August.   5 Why is he walking to and fro?   6 He is walking to and fro because he is nervous.

EXERCISE II

1 Which is the cheaper journey, the one to Holland or the one to Switzerland?   2 The journey to Holland is cheaper.   3 Is this the highest church steeple in Europe?   4 Yes, it is the highest.   5 Have you climbed the stairs and brought down the bicycle?   6 No, I did not bring it down, because I did not find it.

3 There are certain verbs in German which can be used with a particular Preposition. Here is a list of the most useful ones:

zu

Ich gehe zu Fuss.	I am going on foot.
Um wieviel Uhr essen wir zu Mittag?	What time are we having lunch?
Er kaufte ein Paket Zigaretten zu 50 Pfennig.	He bought a packet of cigarettes for 50 pfennigs.

nach

Wir schickten nach dem Arzt.	We sent for the doctor.
Er erkundigte sich nach dem Zug.	He inquired about the train.

über

Ich freue mich über seinen Besuch.	I am pleased about his visit.
Wir sprechen über seinen Brief.	We are talking about his letter.
Sie war sehr traurig über den Tod ihrer Freundin.	She was very sad at the death of her friend.

unter

Unter solchen Umständen kann ich nichts machen.	In such circumstances I can do nothing.
Unter welcher Bedingung wollen Sie ihr helfen?	On what condition will you help her?

um

Sie spielen um Geld.	They are playing for money.
Er bat mich um Rat.	He asked me for advice.

vor

Er zittert vor Kälte.	He is trembling with cold.
Ich habe Angst vor ihm.	I am afraid of him.

für

Ich interessiere mich sehr für die Kunst.	I am very interested in art.

an

Ich denke oft an meine Mutter.	I often think of my mother.
Glauben Sie an diese Geschichte?	Do you believe in this story?
Er leidet an schweren Kopfschmerzen.	He is suffering from severe headache.
Es fehlte ihm an dem notwendigen Geld.	He lacked the necessary money.

auf

Wir fahren auf einige Tage in die Berge.	We are going to the mountains for a few days.
Ich freue mich auf die Ferien.	I am looking forward to the holidays.
Er war sehr stolz auf seine Kenntnisse.	He was very proud of his knowledge.

EXERCISE III

1 Did he ask about the train? 2 Yes, he made the necessary inquiry. 3 Did you speak about his reply? 4 Yes, we spoke about it. 5 Has she asked you for help? 6 No, she did not ask for it. 7 Were you frightened of the dog? 8 No, I was not frightened of it.

NEW WORDS

die Reise (n)	the journey
der Kirchturm (¨e)	the church steeple
die Treppe (n)	the stairs
das Fahrrad (¨er)	the bicycle
herunterbringen (*irreg*)	to bring down
die Erkundigung (en)	the inquiry
die Mansarde (n)	the attic
die Antwort (en)	the answer
der Hund (e)	the dog
Angst haben	to be frightened of
nervös sein	to be nervous
sich erkundigen nach	to inquire about
hin und her	to and fro

Lesson Twenty-Two

1 In English **the subjunctive** is hardly ever used; in German it is essential in some cases. The subjunctive is used in subordinate clauses, in indirect speech, indirect statement or question, or when expressing a wish.

It should be borne in mind that any verb of *saying, asking, declaring, maintaining,* or *believing* may introduce indirect speech. The subjunctive is never used in the imperative or in any main clause where the principal verb is in the present tense. The same applies to sentences in which the exact words of questions and answers are repeated. However, if any doubt of the truth is suggested the subjunctive must be used.

2 Subjunctive of regular and auxiliary verbs

2a: leben—to live

PRESENT SUBJUNCTIVE

ich lebe	**wir leben**
du lebest	**ihr lebet**
er lebe	**Sie leben**
sie lebe	**sie leben**
es lebe	

IMPERFECT SUBJUNCTIVE

ich lebte	**wir lebten**
du lebtest	**ihr lebtet**
er lebte	**Sie lebten**
sie lebte	**sie lebten**
es lebte	

117

ich habe gelebt	wir haben gelebt
du habest gelebt	ihr habet gelebt
er habe gelebt	Sie haben gelebt
sie habe gelebt	sie haben gelebt
es habe gelebt	

This shows that the subjunctive of regular verbs is formed like the indicative except in the 2nd and 3rd person singular and in the 2nd person plural.

2b: haben—to have

PRESENT SUBJUNCTIVE

ich habe	wir haben
du habest	ihr habet
er habe	Sie haben
sie habe	sie haben
es habe	

IMPERFECT SUBJUNCTIVE

ich hätte	wir hätten
du hättest	ihr hättet
er hätte	Sie hätten
sie hätte	sie hätten
es hätte	

PERFECT SUBJUNCTIVE

ich hätte gehabt	wir hätten gehabt
du hättest gehabt	ihr hättet gehabt
er hätte gehabt	Sie hätten gehabt
sie hätte gehabt	sie hätten gehabt
es hätte gehabt	

2c: **sein**—*to be* is also irregular in the present subjunctive.

PRESENT SUBJUNCTIVE

ich sei	wir seien
du seiest	ihr seiet
er sei	Sie seien
sie sei	sie seien
es sei	

IMPERFECT SUBJUNCTIVE

ich wäre	wir wären
du wärest	ihr wäret
er wäre	Sie wären
sie wäre	sie wären
es wäre	

PERFECT SUBJUNCTIVE

ich sei gewesen	wir seien gewesen
du seiest gewesen	ihr seiet gewesen
er sei gewesen	Sie seien gewesen
sie sei gewesen	sie seien gewesen
es sei gewesen	

PLUPERFECT SUBJUNCTIVE

ich wäre gewesen	wir wären gewesen
du wärest gewesen	ihr wäret gewesen
er wäre gewesen	Sie wären gewesen
sie wäre gewesen	sie wären gewesen
es wäre gewesen	

2d The subjunctive of auxiliary verbs retains the umlaut of the infinitive in all tenses. Exceptions are **wollen**—*to want to,* and **sollen**—*shall* or *ought to.*

3 The irregular verbs form their present tense subjunctive like the regular verbs. To the imperfect form add an umlaut to **o, a, u, au** and also an additional **e** to the singular.

119

kommen to come *Imperfect* **kam**—came *Subjunctive* **käme**

ich käme	wir kämen
du kämest	ihr kämet
er käme	Sie kämen
sie käme	sie kämen
es käme	

Verbs which have no **o, a, u, au** in the stem simply add an **e**.

gehen to go *Imperfect* **ging**—went *Subjunctive* **ginge**.

e.g. **Er sagte, er sei müde.**
He said he was tired.
Sie sagte, sie käme heute nicht.
She said she was not coming to-day.

4   Use of subjunctive in **reported speech.**

Sie behauptete, sie stamme aus Amerika.
She maintained that her home country was America.

Note the following examples of reported speech, where the subjunctive is **not** used because the principal verb is in the present tense.

Er fragt, fahren Sie mit.
He asks if you are coming along.
Sie sagt, dass der Buchhalter kommen wird.
She says the accountant is coming.
Ich glaube, es gibt morgen schönes Wetter.
I believe the weather will be fine to-morrow.

5   Use of subjunctive in **indirect questions.**

Wir fragten, ob sie einen Strafzettel bekommen hätte.
We asked whether she had received a parking ticket.

Note the subjunctive used with an auxiliary verb in the indirect question.

120

Ich sagte, ich hätte nicht früher anrufen können.
I said I could not have phoned earlier.
**Er fragte mich, ob ich heute noch Deutsch lehren
    möchte.**
He asked me whether I would still like to teach German today.

6 Use of subjunctive in **expressing a wish.**

Wäre er jetzt nur hier!
If only he were here now.

7 The conjunction **dass** often joins two sentences, in which
case the verb must go to the end of the clause. The conjunction **dass** may however be omitted, in which case the
word order is as usual.

e.g. **Ich glaubte, dass er ein guter Freund wäre, aber das
    stimmte nicht.**
I thought he was a good friend, but it proved not to be the case.

or

Ich glaubte, er wäre ein guter Freund.

EXERCISE I

1 Would you do this in my place?   2 Yes, I would do the
same.   3 Did he say that he had written the report?   4 No,
he did not mention it.   5 Could you let me know whether the
board has come to a decision?   6 Yes, the decision was made
yesterday.

8 In forming a polite question one often uses the subjunctive
of an auxiliary.

e.g. **Dürfte ich das Fenster öffnen?**
Would you mind if I opened the window?
Könnte ich die Rechnung mit Scheck bezahlen?
Could I pay the bill by cheque?

121

EXERCISE II

1 What would you like? 2 I would like a pair of shoes and matching handbag. 3 Could you lend me your binoculars to watch the race? 4 Yes, of course, but please give them back to me soon. 5 Would you like to go to the cinema with me? 6 That is very kind of you, but I would prefer to go to the theatre.

Translate into German:

The driver said he was quite ready. I asked him whether he knew at what time we would arrive. He said he was not sure. On the way we asked a policeman whether we were on the right road. He said he was not certain, but could ask his assistant. The driver thought this was not necessary and we drove on.

CONVERSATIONAL PRACTICE

Bei meinem letzten Besuch in Deutschland fragte mich meine Freundin, was wir jetzt tun sollten.
During my last visit to Germany my girl friend asked me what we should do next.

Ich sagte, dass ich gern in die Geschäfte ginge, um zu sehen, was man hier kaufen könnte.
I said that I would like to go to the shops to see what could be bought.

Die Verkäuferin fragte uns, was für uns in Frage käme.
The sales lady asked us what we would like.

Wir sagten, wir möchten uns nur umschauen.
We said we would merely like to have a look round.

Nach einiger Zeit sagte ich zu der Verkäuferin, ob ich das schwarze Kleid mal anprobieren könnte.
After some time I asked the sales lady whether I could try on the black dress.

122

| Leider war das Kleid zu eng und ich bat meine Freundin, es der Verkäuferin zurückzubringen. Danach verliessen wir das Geschäft. | Unfortunately the dress was too tight and I asked my friend to return it to the sales lady. After that we left the shop. |

NEW WORDS

der Strafzettel (–)	the parking ticket
der Feldstecher (–)	the binoculars
das Rennen (–)	the race
der Mitarbeiter (–)	the assistant
der Ausschuss	the board of directors
den Entschluss fassen	to come to a decision
auf dem Weg, unterwegs	on the way
an meiner Stelle	in my place
was käme für Sie in Frage	what would you like
passend	matching
behaupten	to maintain
stammen aus	to originate from
lehren	to teach
fertig sein	to be ready
nötig sein	to be necessary
sicher sein	to be sure
eng	tight
weiterfahren (*irreg*)	to continue

Lesson Twenty-Three

1 The conditional is formed with **würden** and an infinitive of the verb. However, one often uses the imperfect subjunctive of **haben** and **sein** or the imperfect subjunctive of the verb.

Conditional of **werden—würde**

ich würde	I would	**wir würden**	we would
du würdest	you would	**ihr würdet**	you would
er würde	he would	**Sie würden**	you would
sie würde	she would	**sie würden**	they would
es würde	it would		

e.g. **Was würden Sie ihm schicken?**
What would you send to him?
Ich würde ihm sofort ein Telex schicken.
I would send him a telex at once.
An seiner Stelle ginge ich zum Direktor der Firma.
In his place I would go to the director of the Company.
Ich wäre über diese Neuigkeit nicht sehr erfreut.
I should not be very pleased about this news.

2 The conjunction **wenn**—*if*, which combines two sentences, is often used to express the conditional tense. Just as in English, this word may be followed by a present or future tense, if the sense requires it:

124

INDICATIVE PRESENT TENSE

Wenn er auf dem Flugplatz keinen Koffer-Kuli bekommt, muss er die Koffer selbst tragen.
If he does not get a trolley at the airport he must carry the suitcases himself.

FUTURE TENSE

Wenn er auf dem Flugplatz keinen Koffer-Kuli bekommen wird, wird er die Koffer selbst tragen müssen.
If he can not get a trolley at the airport he will have to carry the suitcases himself.

CONDITIONAL IMPERFECT TENSE

Wenn er auf dem Flugplatz keinen Koffer-Kuli bekäme, müsste er die Koffer selbst tragen.
If he were not able to get a trolley at the airport, he would have to carry the suitcases himself.

PLUPERFECT TENSE

Wenn er auf dem Flugplatz keinen Koffer-Kuli bekommen hätte, hätte er die Koffer selbst tragen müssen.
If he had not been able to get a trolley at the airport he would have had to carry the suitcases himself.

3   Wenn can be omitted in the conditional tense. The word order is then the normal one, but **so** should be included in the subordinate clause.

e.g. **Wenn Sie kein Geld hätten, könnten Sie nicht wegfahren.**
If you had no money you could not travel.

or

Hätten Sie kein Geld, so könnten Sie nicht wegfahren.

125

EXERCISE I

1 Would you buy a car from this man if he were a dealer? 2 No, I do not trust him and would not buy a car from him. 3 Would she have made this trunk call for me, if I had paid for it? 4 I am not sure whether or not she knows the correct dialling code. 5 If he went with you, would you accompany him? 6 No, I would not accompany him, as he is not my type.

4 The word **gern** is used with a verb to mean *to like (to do)*. With **haben**, the meaning is simply *to like*, implying affection, and is used mainly when referring to people. **Gern** is an adverb and is not declined. Also, when ordering a meal or entering a shop one says: **ich hätte gern** or **ich möchte gern,** *I would like*.

Gern geschehen is also a useful phrase meaning *don't mention it*.

e.g. **Er liest gern.**
He likes reading.
Hätten Sie gern noch eine Tasse Tee?
Would you like another cup of tea?
Ich habe meine Freunde sehr gern.
I like my friends very much.
Möchten Sie gern ein Glass Bier?
Would you like a glass of beer?

EXERCISE II

1 If I were to give you my card, could you send me his address? 2 That would be possible. 3 Did your friend break his ankle while skiing? 4 No, had he broken his ankle, he could not have flown back. 5 Would your daughter know what to do with her inheritance? 6 No, she would have no idea how to invest the money.

126

Translate into German:

Would you go with me to a good restaurant if I were to invite you? I would very much like to go if you gave me enough notice. Very well, I could do that. Would it suit you if we were to meet next Friday evening at eight o'clock under the big clock at the main station? That would be very nice, provided nothing happens in the meantime. Would you like me to confirm this arrangement? That would be very kind of you. Many thanks in advance, I am looking forward to the evening.

CONVERSATIONAL PRACTICE

Vor ein paar Tagen wurden wir zum Essen in ein Restaurant eingeladen.

A few days ago we were invited for a meal in a restaurant.

Unser Gastgeber sagte: „was würden Sie denn essen, wenn Geld keine Rolle spielte?"

Our host asked what would we have if money was no object?

Wir lachten und sagten, dass wir in diesem Falle das teuerste bestellen würden.

We laughed and said in that case we would order whatever was most expensive.

„Herr Ober, könnten Sie uns die Speisekarte bringen?"

"Waiter, could you bring us the menu?"

„Ich würde Ihnen gern eine bringen, wenn ich eine hätte."

"I would gladly bring you one, if I had one."

„Aber vielleicht könnten Sie sich auch ohne Karte etwas aussuchen."

"You could perhaps choose something without one."

Wir überlegten lange, dann fragten wir, ob wir das billigste Essen haben könnten.

We thought for a long time and then we asked whether we could have the cheapest meal.

Nach einem guten und reichhaltigen Essen rief unser Freund: „Herr Ober, wir möchten zahlen.“	After a good and substantial meal our friend called to the waiter: "Waiter, could we have the bill, please."
Wir waren etwas erstaunt aber wir waren gern bereit die Rechnung zu teilen.	We were rather surprised but we were quite prepared to share the bill.
Das Essen kostete DM. 80.00, dazu kamen die Bedienung mit 15% und die Mehrwertsteuer mit 12%.	The meal was DM. 80.00 plus 15% service and 12% VAT.
Wir bedankten uns bei dem Kellner und gingen weg.	We thanked the waiter and departed.

NEW WORDS

das Telex	the telex
der Koffer Kuli (–)	the trolley
der Händler (–)	the dealer
der Fernanruf (e)	the trunk call
die Vorwählnummer (n)	the dialling code
die Besuchskarte (n)	the (visiting) card
der Knöchel (–)	the ankle
die Erbschaft (en)	the inheritance
die Verabredung (en)	the arrangement
der Gastgeber (–)	the host
die Speisekarte)n)	the menu
der Typ (en)	the type
die Bedienung	the service
die Mehrwertsteuer	the VAT
Bescheid geben	to give notice
das Prozent (e)	the percentage

das Skifahren	the skiing
begleiten	to accompany
anlegen	to invest money
bestätigen	to confirm
aufmerksam sein	to be kind
im voraus	in advance
aussuchen	to select, choose
reichhaltig	substantial
trauen (+*dat.*)	to trust

Lesson Twenty-Four

1 Some **impersonal verbs** govern **the accusative case.**
Here is a list of the most important ones:

es wundert mich	I am surprised
es freut mich	I am pleased
es friert mich	I am cold
es ärgert mich	I am annoyed

2 There are some which govern **the dative case:**

es fehlt mir an	I lack
es gelingt mir	I succeed
es schwindelt mir	I am dizzy
es eilt mir	I am in a hurry

3 To talk of **the weather** one uses similar expressions to
English:

es regnet	it is raining
es friert	it is freezing
es donnert	it is thundering
es blitzt	it is lightning
es taut	it is thawing

But one uses the dative case in the following expressions:

mir ist kalt	I am cold
mir ist warm	I am warm

Most of these verbs are weak and decline in the perfect tense
regularly with **haben**, except **gelingen**—*to succeed* and **frieren**
—*to freeze,* which decline with **sein**—*to be,* in the perfect tense.

130

e.g. **Ich habe mich über seinen Brief sehr gefreut.**
I was very pleased with his letter.
Er hat sich über ihr Benehmen sehr geärgert.
He was very annoyed about her behaviour.
Hat es gestern nacht stark geregnet?
Did it rain heavily last night?
Mir war im letzten Winter sehr kalt gewesen.
I felt very cold last winter.
**Ist es Ihnen gelungen diesen Artikel auf der Messe
zu verkaufen?**
Did you succeed in selling this article at the trade fair?

4 In order to use **es gibt, es sind**—*there is, there are,* correctly,
a few points need to be explained.

If the number is not specified use **es gibt.**

e.g. **Es gibt viele Leute auf dem Bahnhof.**
There are many people at the station.
Es gibt heute keine Milch.
There is no milk to-day.

But if the amount is specified use **es ist, es sind,**—*there is,
there are.*

e.g. **Es ist ein Pfund Butter im Kühlschrank.**
There is a pound of butter in the refrigerator.
Es sind dreissig Stühle in der Klasse.
There are thirty chairs in the class room.

5 **The present participle** and the **adjectival adjunct** are
both formed by adding a **d** to the Infinitive of the verb. The
present participle is used as in English (except that there is no
equivalent of the English form of the present tense *I am reading*).

e.g. **Kopfschüttelnd verliess er das Zimmer.**
Shaking his head he left the room.

or

**Er schüttelte den Kopf, indem er das Zimmer
verliess.**
He shook his head when he left the room.

131

The adjectival adjunct is a long adjectival clause and it precedes the noun. It is declined like an ordinary adjective plus the added **d.**

e.g. **Ich hörte die singenden, zwitschernden Vögel auf den Bäumen.**
I heard the singing, twittering birds in the trees.

EXERCISE I

1 Was he surprised to get this unexpected present? 2 No, but I was very pleased about it. 3 When you were ill, were you dizzy? 4 Yes, I am still occasionally very dizzy. 5 Are the teachers short of money? 6 No, they are very well paid at present.

EXERCISE II

1 Is there a particularly interesting museum in your town? 2 Yes, there are many. 3 Is there a ready-baked cake in the deep-freeze? 4 No, I did not bake one to-day. 5 Does the continuous rainy weather annoy you? 6 Yes, and the slippery roads are very dangerous.

6 In addition to the ordinary way of using possessive adjectives like **mein, dein, sein,** etc. one can use these words to stand in place of a noun, and they must be declined, like nouns. This way one does not need to repeat the same noun in the same sentence.

e.g. **Mein Bleistift und seiner.**
My pencil and his.
Wenn Sie Ihren Bleistift vergessen haben, nehmen Sie doch den meinigen.
If you have forgotten your pencil, do take mine.

or

Wenn Sie Ihren Bleistift vergessen haben, nehmen Sie doch meinen.

If you have forgotten your pencil, do take mine.

EXERCISE III

1 Whom can one meet on the way home at 11 o'clock at night? 2 One can meet the singing, noisy people who come out of the pub. 3. Whom does he like best? 4 He likes best of all the giggling and laughing girls. 5 Is that the same newspaper as mine? 6 No, it is not the same. 7 What has happened to our dog? 8 I have not seen yours anywhere.

5 A number of adjectives or adverbs form the negative by prefixing **un**. Here are a few:

freundlich	kind	**unfreundlich**	unfriendly
ruhig	quiet	**unruhig**	restless
sichtbar	visible	**unsichtbar**	invisible
wichtig	important	**unwichtig**	unimportant
gemütlich	cosy, snug	**ungemütlich**	unpleasant

e.g. **Er antwortete auf eine unfreundliche Art.**
He answered in an unfriendly manner.
War die Wohnung gemütlich?
Was the apartment cosy?
Nein, es war eine sehr ungemütliche Wohnung.
No, it was not a very pleasant flat.

CONVERSATIONAL PRACTICE

Waren Sie kürzlich einkaufen gewesen?
Have you been shopping recently?
Ja, ich musste mir Schuhe und neue Kleider für den Sommer anschaffen.
Yes, I had to buy new shoes and new dresses for the summer.

133

Hatten Sie Schwierig- keiten, die richtige Grösse zu bekommen?	Did you have any difficulties in getting the right size?
Ja, zuerst fand ich es fast unmöglich, mich zwischen den englischen und den kontinentalen Grössen zurechtzufinden.	Yes, at first I found it almost impossible to find my way around the English and the Continental sizes.
Ich bin froh, dass heute beide Grössen auf dem Etikett sichtbar sind, so dass es leichter ist die richtige Grösse einzukaufen.	I am glad that both sizes are mentioned on the label now, so that it is easier to shop for the correct size.
Ist das nur wichtig in der Damenkleidung oder auch für die Männer?	Does that only apply to ladies' clothes, or also to men's clothes?
Nein, das gleiche gilt auch für die Männerkleidung.	No, the same applies to men's clothing.
Vielen Dank.	Mank thanks.
Es war sehr freundlich von Ihnen mir das zu erklären.	It was very kind of you to explain it to me.
Gern geschehen.	Don't mention it.

NEW WORDS

das Benehmen	the behaviour
die Messe (n)	the trade fair
der Kühlschrank ("e)	the refrigerator
das Geschenk (e)	the present
die Tiefkühltruhe (n)	the deep freeze
die Wirtschaft (en)	the pub
die Kneipe (n)	the pub
der Hund (e)	the dog
die Art, die Weise (en, n)	the manner
die Grösse (n)	the size

das Etikett (e)	the label
das Museum, die Museen	the museum
der Heimweg (e)	the way home
schütteln	to shake
zwitschern	to twitter
unerwartet	unexpected
backen, er bäckt (*irreg*)	to bake
anschaffen (*irreg*)	to buy
zurechtfinden (*irreg*)	to find one's way
kichern	to giggle
gelten, es gilt	to be valid
krank	sick
glatt, schlüpfrig	slippery
gefährlich	dangerous
ununterbrochen	continuous
lärmend	noisy

GERMAN
IN THREE MONTHS

II

IDIOMS & READING TEXTS

VOCABULARIES

Introduction

Having worked through the grammar lessons in Part I and mastered the basic constructions of the language, the reader will be looking for help with the everyday colloquial expressions that are so necessary for a working grasp of conversational German. Obviously it is impossible to include an exhaustive collection of German idioms: there is space here to give only some of the most common and most useful. The learner should read these aloud (after listening to the recording if possible), and imagine situations in which he might use them. He would do well to select those he considers most useful and then learn them by heart.

Following the idioms there is a handful of extracts from some well-known modern German writers. One of the great satisfactions of learning a foreign language is that a new literature becomes available. You should get into the habit of reading German as soon as possible, and there is no reason for not starting with the best. We hope these extracts will show you something—a very small something—of what German literature has to offer. The English translations on the opposite page should be referred to as little as possible, and we suggest you try reading the German pieces aloud.

Idiomatic Expressions

Aus den Augen verlieren.	*Out of sight, out of mind.*
Ohne allen Anlass.	*For no reason at all.*
Es kommt darauf an.	*It depends.*
Anwesende ausgenommen.	*Present company excepted.*
Er ist auch nur ein Mensch.	*He is nothing but a human being.*
Ich kann mich nicht damit aufhalten.	*I can not waste my time on it.*
Mir geht ein Licht auf.	*I begin to see daylight.*
Keinen aufkommen lassen.	*Admit no rival.*
Sein Auskommen haben.	*To make one's living.*
Nach dem Aussehen urteilen.	*To judge by appearances.*
Ausser Zweifel.	*Beyond all doubt.*
Sich etwas anders überlegen.	*To change one's mind.*
Schwer von Begriff.	*To be dense.*
Stunden nehmen.	*To take lessons.*
Zum Wohl.	*To your health.*
Was mich anbelangt.	*What concerns me.*
Über alle Berge sein.	*To be off and away.*
Bescheid geben.	*To let a person know.*
Jemanden zur Besinnung bringen.	*To bring a person to his senses.*
Ein Mann in den besten Jahren.	*A man in the prime of life.*
Es kommt nicht in Frage.	*Out of the question.*
In Bezug auf.	*With regard to.*
Kein Blatt vor den Mund nehmen.	*Not to mince matters.*
Es bleibt dabei.	*Agreed.*

In die Brüche gehen.	To come to grief.
Sie treibt es zu bunt.	She goes too far.
Was ist denn dabei?	What harm is there?
Jemanden zum Dank verpflichtet sein.	To be obliged to a person.
Ich bin daran.	It is my turn.
Sie sind darüber weg.	You are over it.
Auf die Dauer.	In the long run.
Dicke Luft.	Trouble is brewing.
Mir dreht sich der Kopf.	My head swims.
Er spricht dummes Zeug.	He talks nonsense.
Das ist ein durchgehender Zug.	This is a through train.
Wie ein rohes Ei behandeln.	Handle with kid gloves.
Es lässt sich einrichten.	It can be arranged.
Ich liess das Telefon mindestens fünf Minuten klingeln, aber das Fräulein vom Amt sagte es sei keine Antwort.	I let the telephone ring for at least five minutes but the operator told me there was no reply.
Die Tür ist nur angelehnt.	The door is ajar.
Haben Sie die Schuhe zum Schuhmacher gebracht?	Did you bring the shoes to the shoemaker?
Ist das das erste Mal?	Is this the first time?
Nein, das ist das zweite Mal.	No, it is the second time.
Er gab es mir letztes Mal.	He gave it to me last time.
Welchen Weg muss ich gehen? Rechts oder links?	Which way must I go? To the right or to the left?
Nein, gehen Sie geradeaus.	No, carry straight on.
Haben Sie gut geschlafen?	Did you sleep well?
Nein, ich bin mehrmals aufgewacht.	No, I woke up several times.
Das kommt mir gerade recht.	That comes in handy.
Ans Herz wachsen.	To grow fond of.
Der Motor springt nicht an.	The engine won't start.
Jemanden im Auto mitnehmen.	To give somebody a lift.
Ich denke nicht daran.	I would not think of it.

141

Was fehlt Ihnen denn?	*What is the matter with you?*
Ich habe Kopfschmerzen.	*I have a headache.*
Das macht mir nichts aus.	*I do not mind.*
Unterm Pantoffel stehen.	*To be tied to somebody's apron string.*
Aus guter Quelle haben.	*To have it on good authority.*
Er hat keine Lust.	*He does not feel like it.*
Das Gespräch in Gang bringen.	*To start the ball rolling.*
Davon kann keine Rede sein.	*That is out of the question.*
Ein Leben führen.	*To live a life.*
Seinen Einfluss geltend machen.	*To bring one's influence to bear.*
Gute Miene zum bösen Spiel machen.	*Grin and bear it.*
Wenn es nach mir ginge.	*If I had my way.*
Gesund und munter.	*Fit as a fiddle.*
Darauf können Sie Gift nehmen.	*You bet your life on it.*
Es ist mein voller Ernst.	*I mean it.*
Jemanden in die Rede fallen.	*To interrupt somebody.*
Ich habe es für mein Leben gern.	*I am exceedingly fond of it.*
Ich lasse es mir nicht gefallen.	*I will not stand for it.*
Das können Sie halten wie Sie wollen.	*You can please yourself.*
Es hapert noch.	*There is something amiss.*
Sich die Hörner abstossen.	*To sow one's wild oats.*
Ich kann nicht klug daraus werden.	*I cannot make head or tail of it.*
Von der Hand weisen.	*To reject.*
In die Klappe gehen.	*Go to bed.*
Bitte sprechen Sie Deutsch; ich spreche kein Englisch.	*Speak German please; I do not understand English.*
Möchten Sie Ihren Mantel ablegen?	*Would you like to take your coat off?*
In welchem Teil von London wohnen Sie?	*In what part of London do you live?*

Haben Sie sonst noch was zu fragen?	*Have you anything else to ask?*
Wollen Sie dies einpacken?	*Will you pack this up?*
Sie gehen nicht genug an die frische Luft.	*You don't have enough fresh air.*
Ich habe keine Zeit, mir Bewegung zu machen; ich muss viel studieren.	*I have no time for exercise; I have to study a great deal.*
Man kann Zeit zu allem finden, wenn man sich richtig einrichtet.	*One can find time for everything if one plans things properly.*
Nicht jeder hat soviel Willenskraft wie Sie.	*Everyone has not as much willpower as you have.*
Machen Sie sich über mich lustig oder schmeicheln Sie mir?	*Are you making fun of me or are you flattering me?*
Keines von beiden; ich spreche nur die Wahrheit.	*Neither; I am merely saying what is true.*
Haben Sie sich nicht um die Sache gekümmert?	*Haven't you looked into the matter?*
Wollen Sie diese Papiere ordnen?	*Will you put these papers in order?*
Ich habe sie erst letzte Woche geordnet.	*I arranged them only last week.*
Sie sind dennoch schon wieder ganz in Unordnung.	*Nevertheless, they are completely out of order.*
Ich möchte wissen, wer der Schuldige ist.	*I should like to know who the guilty party is.*
„Verboten" ist ein sehr wichtiges Wort in Deutschland.	*"Forbidden" is a very important word in Germany.*
Eingang verboten.	*No admittance.*
Rauchen verboten.	*No smoking (allowed here).*
Überschreiten der Geleise verboten.	*It is forbidden to cross the lines.*
Unbefugten ist der Eintritt verboten.	*No trespassers.*

143

Sie wollten heute früh mit mir sprechen.	You wanted to speak to me this morning.
Sie können es jetzt tun, wenn es Ihnen passt.	You can do so now, if it suits you.
Es ist nichts sehr Wichtiges, es ist besser, es während der Geschäftsstunden zu besprechen.	It is nothing very important; it is better to talk it over in business hours.
In gutem Einvernehmen sein.	To be on friendly terms.
Zu Ende gehen.	Come to an end (is over).
Sich elend fühlen.	To feel miserable.
In die engere Wahl kommen.	To be on the short list.
Über sich ergehen lassen.	To submit to.
Es fehlt mir an Geld.	I am lacking in money.
Morgen ist auch ein Tag.	To-morrow is another day.
Sie müssen die Folgen tragen.	You must bear the consequences.
Er wurde auf frischer Tat ertappt.	He was caught red-handed.
Ich könnte aus der Haut fahren.	I almost jumped out of my skin.
Sie will den Haushalt führen.	She wants to keep house.
Bitte sprechen Sie langsamer.	Please speak more slowly.
Sie sprechen viel zu schnell für mich.	You speak must too fast for me.
Es ist nichts mehr übrig.	There is nothing left.
Kann ich den Chef sprechen?	Can I see the principal (the boss)?
Bitte sagen Sie mir, was Sie von ihm wollen?	Please tell me why you want to see him?
Gut, ich werde Sie anmelden.	Very well, I will take your card in.
Herr H. bedauert, aber er kann Sie heute nicht sehen.	Mr. H. regrets that he can not see you to-day.
Finden Sie deutsch leicht oder schwer?	Do you find German easy or difficult?
Ich finde es nicht schwer.	I do not find it very difficult.

Zuerst waren Sie zufrieden ganz einfache Sätze zu machen.	*At first you were content to make simple sentences.*
Jetzt sind Sie ehrgeizig und versuchen fliessend zu sprechen.	*Now you are ambitious and attempt to speak fluently.*
Das stimmt, aber man muss versuchen weiterzukommen.	*That is so, but one must try to make progress.*
Erlauben Sie mir, etwas zu fragen?	*Allow me to ask something.*
Gestatten Sie ihm zu sprechen.	*Permit him to speak.*
Nehmen Sie doch Platz!	*Do take a seat!*
Nein danke, ich kann nicht zu lange bleiben.	*No thank you, I cannot stay too long.*
Wollen Sie so freundlich sein, es für mich zu besorgen?	*Will you be so kind as to see to it for me?*

Reading Texts

GESPRÄCH MIT EINEM OFEN

Er stellte sich mir vor: dick, breit, das große Maul voll Feuer.
„Ich heiße Franklin", sagte er.
„Bist du Benjamin Franklin?" fragte ich.
„Nein, nur Franklin. Oder Francolino. Ich bin ein italienischer Ofen, eine vorzügliche Erfindung. Ich wärme zwar nicht besonders—"
„Ja", sagte ich, „das ist mir bekannt. Alle Öfen mit schönen Namen sind vorzügliche Erfindungen, heizen aber mäßig. Ich liebe sie sehr, sie verdienen Bewunderung. Aber sage, Franklin, wie kommt das, daß ein italienischer Ofen einen amerikanischen Namen hat? Ist das nicht sonderbar?"
„Sonderbar? Nein, das ist eines der geheimen Gesetze, weißt du. Ein geheimes Gesetz der Beziehungen und Ergänzungen, die Natur ist ja voll von solchen Gesetzen. Die feigen Völker haben Volkslieder, in denen der Mut verherrlicht wird. Die lieblosen Völker haben Theaterstücke, in denen die Liebe verherrlicht wird. So ist es auch mit uns, mit uns Öfen. Ein italienischer Ofen heißt meistens amerikanisch, so wie ein deutscher Ofen meistens griechisch heißt. Sie sind deutsch, und glaube mir, sie wärmen um nichts besser als ich, aber sie heißen Heureka oder Phönix oder Hektors Abschied. Es weckt große Erinnerungen. So heiße auch ich Franklin. Ich bin ein Ofen, aber ich könnte, nach manchen Kennzeichen, ebensogut ein Staatsmann sein. Ich habe einen großen Mund, verbrauche viel, wärme wenig, speie Rauch durch ein Rohr, trage einen guten Namen und wecke große Erinnerungen. So ist das mit mir."

CONVERSATION WITH A STOVE

He introduced himself, large, wide, his big mouth full of fire.
"My name is Franklin," he said.
"Are you Benjamin Franklin?" I asked.
"No, only Franklin. Or Francolino. I am an Italian stove, an excellent invention. I admit that I do not prove a lot of warmth—".
"Yes", I said, "I know that. All stoves with beautiful names are excellent inventions but heat only moderately well. I am very fond of them, they deserve admiration. But tell me Franklin, why is it that an Italian stove has an American name? Is that not strange?"
"Strange? No, don't you know it is one of the secret laws. A secret law of relationships and additions. Nature is full of such secret laws. The cowardly nations have folk songs in which courage is praised. Cold (unloving) nations have plays in which love is exalted. It is the same with us, with us ovens. An Italian stove has usually got an American name in the same way as a German stove has usually a Greek one. They are German, and believe me, they heat no better than me, but they are called Heureka or Phönix or Hektor's Farewell. It awakens strong memories. That is why I am called Franklin. I am a stove, but because of certain characteristics, I could also be a statesman. I have got a big mouth, consume a lot, provide little warmth, emit smoke through a pipe, bear a good name and awaken vivid memories. That is what I am like."

147

„Gewiß", sagte ich, „ich habe die größte Achtung vor Ihnen. Da Sie ein italienischer Ofen sind, kann man gewiß auch Kastanien in Ihnen braten?"

„Man kann es, gewiß. Es ist ein Zeitvertreib. Viele lieben das. Manche machen auch Verse, oder spielen Schach. Gewiß kann man auch Kastanien in mir braten, warum nicht? Sie verbrennen zwar, aber der Zeitvertreib ist da. Die Menschen lieben den Zeitvertreib, und ich bin Menschenwerk. Wir tun eben unsre Pflicht, wir Denkmäler, nicht mehr nicht weniger."

„Warten Sie! ,Denkmäler'—sagen Sie? Betrachten Sie sich als ein Denkmal?"

„Aber ja. Wir alle sind Denkmäler. Wir Erzeugnisse der Industrie sind alle Denkmäler einer menschlichen Eigenschaft oder Tugend, einer Eigenschaft, welche in der Natur selten ist und in höherer Ausbildung sich nur beim Menschen findet."

„Welche Eigenschaft ist das, bitte?"

„Der Sinn für das Unzweckmäßige. Ich bin, neben vielem anderem, ein Denkmal dieses Sinnes. Ich heiße Franklin, ich bin ein Ofen, ich habe einen großen Mund, der das Holz frißt, und ein großes Rohr, durch welches die Wärme den raschesten Weg ins Freie findet. Ich habe auch Ornamente, und ich habe zwei Klappen, die man öffnen und schließen kann. Auch dies ist ein hübscher Zeitvertreib. Man kann damit spielen, wie mit einer Flöte."

„Sie entzücken mich, Franklin. Sie sind der klügste Ofen, den ich je gesehen habe. Aber wie ist das nun: sind Sie nun eigentlich ein Ofen, oder ein Denkmal?"

„Wieviel Sie fragen! Ist es Ihnen nicht bekannt, daß der Mensch das einzige Wesen ist, das den Dingen einen „Sinn" beilegt? Für die ganze Natur ist die Eiche eine Eiche, der Wind ein Wind, das Feuer ein Feuer. Für den Menschen aber ist alles anders, ist alles sinnvoll, alles beziehungsvoll! Alles wird ihm heilig, alles Symbol. Ein Totschlag ist eine Heldentat, eine Seuche ist Gottes Finger, ein Krieg ist Evolution. Wie sollte da ein Ofen nur ein Ofen sein können?! Nein, auch er ist Symbol, er ist Denkmal, er ist Verkünder. Darum liebt man ihn, darum zollt man ihm Achtung. Darum hat er Ornamente und

"Certainly" I said, "I have got the greatest respect for you. As you are an Italian stove, I suppose one can roast chestnuts in you?"

"You can, certainly. It is a pastime. Many people like that. Many compose verses or play chess. Certainly you can roast chestnuts in me; why not? Of course they burn, but it is still a pastime. People love pastimes and I am a human creation. We just do our duty, we monuments, no more, no less."

"Wait a moment! Monuments, did you say? Do you regard yourself as a monument?"

"But of course, we are all monuments. We products of industry are all monuments to a human property or virtue, a property which is seldom found in nature and among the highest species is peculiar to human beings.'

"What property is that please?"

"The delight in impractical things. I am apart from other things, a monument to this faculty. I am called Franklin, I am a stove, I have a big mouth, which devours wood, and a large pipe, through which the warmth finds the quickest way into the open air. I have also got ornaments, and I have got two doors which you can open and shut. That too is a pastime. You can play that like a flute."

"You enchant me, Franklin. You are the cleverest stove I have ever seen. But how can this be: are you really a stove or a monument?"

"What a lot of questions you ask. Don't you know that mankind is the only being which attaches a meaning to things? For the whole of nature an oak tree is an oak tree, the wind a wind, the fire a fire. For mankind however, everything is different, everything is meaningful and connected! Everything becomes holy to him, everything is symbolic. A death blow is a heroic deed, a plague is the hand of God, a war is evolution. How can a stove only be a stove?! No, he too is a symbol, he is a monument, he is a messenger. That is why he is loved and held in esteem. That is why he has got ornaments and doors. That is why he does not see a little bit of heat as his only purpose. That is why he is called Franklin."

149

Klappen. Darum sieht er in dem bißchen Heizen nicht seine einzige Bestimmung. Darum heißt er Franklin."

HERMANN HESSE (1877–1962)

DIE DREI DUNKLEN KÖNIGE

Er tappte durch die dunkle Vorstadt. Die Häuser standen abgebrochen gegen den Himmel. Der Mond fehlte und das Pflaster war erschrocken über den späten Schritt. Dann fand er eine alte Planke. Da trat er mit dem Fuß gegen, bis eine Latte morsch aufseufzte und losbrach. Das Holz roch mürbe und süß. Durch die dunkle Vorstadt tappte er zurück. Sterne waren nicht da.

Als er die Tür aufmachte (sie weinte dabei, die Tür), sahen ihm die blaßblauen Augen seiner Frau entgegen. Sie kamen aus einem müden Gesicht. Ihr Atem hing weiß im Zimmer, so kalt war es. Er beugte sein knochiges Knie und brach das Holz. Das Holz seufzte. Dann roch es mürbe und süß ringsum. Er hielt sich ein Stück davon unter die Nase. „Riecht beinahe wie Kuchen," lachte er leise. „Nicht," sagten die Augen der Frau, „nicht lachen. Er schläft."

Der Mann legte das süße mürbe Holz in den kleinen Blechofen. Da glomm es auf und warf eine Handvoll warmes Licht durch das Zimmer. Die fiel hell auf ein winziges rundes Gesicht und blieb einen Augenblick. Das Gesicht war erst eine Stunde alt, aber es hatte schon alles, was dazugehört: Ohren, Nase, Mund und Augen. Die Augen mußten groß sein, das konnte man sehen, obgleich sie zu waren. Aber der Mund war offen und es pustete leise daraus. Nase und Ohren waren rot. Er lebt, dachte die Mutter. Und das kleine Gesicht schlief.

„Da sind noch Haferflocken," sagte der Mann. „Ja," antwortete die Frau, „das ist gut. Es ist kalt." Der Mann nahm noch von dem süßen weichen Holz. Nun hat sie ihr Kind gekriegt und muß frieren, dachte er. Aber er hatte keinen, dem er dafür die Fäuste ins Gesicht schlagen konnte. Als er die

THE THREE DARK KINGS

He groped his way through the dark suburb. The houses stood in a broken line against the sky. The moon was absent and the pavement was frightened by the late step. Then he found an old plank. He kicked against it with his foot until a lath gave a rotten sigh and broke loose. The wood smelled rotted and sweet. Through the dark suburb he groped his way back. There were no stars.

When he opened the door (it wept as he did so, the door), the pale blue eyes of his wife looked towards him. They came from a tired face. Her breath clung white in the room, it was so cold. He bent his bony knee and broke the wood. The wood sighed. Then there was a rotting and sweet smell about them. He held a piece of it under his nose. "Almost smells like cake," he laughed softly. "No," said his wife's eyes, "don't laugh. He's asleep."

The man placed the sweet, rotting wood in the small tin stove. There it flamed up and cast a handful of warm light through the room. This fell brightly on a tiny round face and stayed there for a moment. The face was only an hour old but it already had everything that belongs to a face: ears, nose, mouth and eyes. The eyes must be big, one could see that, although they were closed. But the mouth was open and a gentle puffing came from it. The nose and ears were red. He lives, the mother thought. And the little face slept.

"There's some rolled oats left," said the man. "Yes," his wife replied, "that's good. It's cold." The man took some more of the sweet, soft wood. Now she's had her child and must be freezing, he thought. But he had no one whose face he could bash in with his fist for that. When he opened the door

151

Ofentür aufmachte, fiel wieder eine Handvoll Licht über das schlafende Gesicht. Die Frau sagte leise: „Kuck, wie ein Heiligenschein, siehst du?" Heiligenschein! dachte er und er hatte keinen, dem er die Fäuste ins Gesicht schlagen konnte.

Dann waren welche an der Tür. „Wir sahen das Licht," sagten sie, „vom Fenster. Wir wollen uns zehn Minuten hinsetzen." „Aber wir haben ein Kind," sagte der Mann zu ihnen. Da sagten sie nichts weiter, aber sie kamen doch ins Zimmer, stießen Nebel aus den Nasen und hoben die Füße hoch. „Wir sind ganz leise," flüsterten sie und hoben die Füße hoch. Dann fiel das Licht auf sie.

Drei waren es. In drei alten Uniformen. Einer hatte einen Pappkarton, einer einen Sack. Und der dritte hatte keine Hände, „Erfroren," sagte er, und hielt die Stümpfe hoch. Dann drehte er dem Mann die Manteltasche hin. Tabak war darin und dünnes Papier. Sie drehten Zigaretten. Aber die Frau sagte: „Nicht, das Kind."

Da gingen die vier vor die Tür und ihre Zigaretten waren vier Punkte in der Nacht. Der eine hatte dicke umwickelte Füße. Er nahm ein Stück Holz aus seinem Sack. „Ein Esel," sagte er, „ich habe sieben Monate daran geschnitzt. Für das Kind." Das sagte er und gab es dem Mann. „Was ist mit den Füßen?" fragte der Mann. „Wasser,"* sagte der Eselschnitzer, „vom Hunger." „Und der andere, der dritte?" fragte der Mann und befühlte im Dunkeln den Esel. Der dritte zitterte in seiner Uniform: „Oh, nichts," wisperte er, „das sind nur die Nerven. Man hat eben zuviel Angst gehabt." Dann traten sie die Zigaretten aus und gingen wieder hinein.

Sie hoben die Füße hoch und sahen auf das kleine schlafende Gesicht. Der Zitternde nahm aus seinem Pappkarton zwei gelbe Bonbons und sagte dazu: „Für die Frau sind die."

Die Frau machte die blassen blauen Augen weit auf, als sie die drei Dunklen über das Kind gebeugt sah. Sie fürchtete sich.

---

* *Wasser:* an edema or swelling caused by an abnormal accumulation of fluid in some part of the body.

of the stove another handful of light fell over the sleeping face. The woman said softly: "Look, like a halo, do you see?" Halo! he thought, and he had no one whose face he could bash in with his fist.

Then there were some people at the door. "We saw the light," they said, "from the window. We want to sit down for ten minutes." "But we have a child," the man said to them. They said nothing more, but they came into the room all the same, breathed mist out of their noses and lifted their feet high. "We'll be very quiet," they whispered and lifted up their feet. Then the light fell on them.

There were three of them. In three old uniforms. One had a cardboard box, one a sack. And the third one had no hands. "Frozen off," he said holding up his stumps. Then he turned the pocket of his overcoat to the man. There was tobacco in it and thin paper. They rolled cigarettes. But the woman said: "No, the child."

So the four of them went outside the door and their cigarettes were four points in the night. One of them had his feet in thick wrappings. He took a piece of wood out of his sack. "A donkey," he said, "I carved at it for seven months. For the child." He said that and gave it to the man. "What's up with your feet?" the man asked. "Water," said the donkey-carver, "from hunger." "And the other, the third one?" the man asked and felt the donkey in the dark. The third man was trembling in his uniform. "Oh, nothing," he whispered, "it's only my nerves. I've simply had too much anxiety." Then they put out their cigarettes and went in again.

They lifted their feet high and looked at the small sleeping face. The trembling man took two yellow candies out of his cardboard box and said: "These are for your wife."

The women opened her pale eyes wide when she saw the three dark men bending over the child. She was afraid. But

Aber da stemmte das Kind seine Beine gegen ihre Brust und schrie so kräftig, daß die drei Dunklen die Füße aufhoben und zur Tür schlichen. Hier nickten sie nochmal, dann stiegen sie in die Nacht hinein.

Der Mann sah ihnen nach. „Sonderbare Heilige," sagte er zu seiner Frau. Dann machte er die Tür zu. „Schöne Heilige sind das," brummte er und sah nach den Haferflocken. Aber er hatte kein Gesicht für seine Fäuste.

„Aber das Kind has geschrien," flüsterte die Frau, „ganz stark hat es geschrien. Da sind sie gegangen. Kuck mal, wie lebendig es ist," sagte sie stolz. Das Gesicht machte den Mund auf und schrie.

„Weint er?" fragte der Mann.

„Nein, ich glaube, er lacht," antwortete die Frau.

„Beinahe wie Kuchen," sagte der Mann und roch an dem Holz, „wie Kuchen. Ganz süß."

„Heute ist ja auch Weihnachten," sagte die Frau.

„Ja, Weihnachten," brummte er und vom Ofen her fiel eine Handvoll Licht hell auf das kleine schlafende Gesicht.

WOLFGANG BORCHERT
(1922–1947)

DAS WARTEN AUF HEDWIG

Es war Montag, der 14. März, und Hedwig kam nicht. Ich hielt die Armbanduhr an mein linkes Ohr und hörte den höhnischen Fleiss des kleinen Zeigers, der Löcher ins Nichts fräste, dunkle, kreisrunde Löcher, die vor meinen Augen zu tanzen begannen, sich um die Haustür herumgruppierten, sich wieder lösten und im blassen Himmel untergingen wie Münzen, die man ins Wasser wirft; dann wieder war für Augenblicke mein Blickfeld durchlöchert wie eins der Bleche, aus denen ich in Wickwebers Fabrik die viereckigen Nickel-

154

at that moment the child dug its legs into her chest and cried so vigorously that the three dark men lifted up their feet and crept to the door. Here they nodded once more, then they went out into the night.

The man looked after them. "Queer saints," he said to his wife. Then he shut the door. "Fine saints they are," he grumbled and looked after the rolled oats. But he had no face for his fists.

"But the child cried," the woman whispered, "it cried quite hard. Then they went. Just look how alive it is," she said proudly. The face opened its mouth and cried.

"Is he crying?" the man asked.

"No, I think he's laughing," the woman replied.

"Almost like cake," said the man and smelled the wood, "like cake. Quite sweet."

"Why it's Christmas today," said the woman.

"Yes, Christmas," he grumbled and from the stove a handful of light fell brightly on the little sleeping face.

Transl. WOLFGANG BORCHERT

WAITING FOR HEDWIG

It was Monday, 14 March, and still Hedwig did not come. I held the wristwatch to my left ear and heard the mocking sound of the busy small hand boring holes in the void, dark circular holes which began to dance before my eyes, drew together round the front door, then broke up again and were lost in the pale sky like stones thrown into the water; then once again my field of vision was perforated like one of the metal sheets from which I had punched four-cornered nickel discs

scheiben ausgestanzt hatte, und ich sah in jedem dieser Löcher die Haustür, sah sie hundertmal, immer dieselbe Haustür, winzige, aber präzise Haustüren, die aneinander hingen in den dünnen Verzahnungen wie Briefmarken auf einem grossen Bogen: hundertmal das Gesicht des Erfinders der Zündkerze.

Hilflos suchte ich in meinen Taschen nach Zigaretten, obwohl ich wusste, dass ich keine mehr hatte, wohl noch eine Packung im Auto lag, aber das Auto stand zwanzig Meter rechts von der Haustür, und etwas wie ein Ozean lag zwischen mir und dem Auto. Und ich dachte wieder an die Frau in der Kurbelstrasse, die geweint hatte am Telefon, wie nur Frauen weinen, die mit Maschinen nicht fertig werden, und ich wusste plötzlich, dass es keinen Zweck mehr hatte, an Ulla vorbeizudenken, und ich dachte an sie; ich tat es, wie man sich plötzlich entschliesst, Licht anzuknipsen in einem Zimmer, in dem jemand gestorben ist: der Dämmer hat ihn noch wie einen Schlafenden erscheinen lassen, und man konnte sich einreden, ihn noch atmen zu hören, seine Bewegungen zu sehen; aber nun fällt das Licht grell auf die Szenerie, und man sieht, dass die Vorbereitungen für die Trauerfeier schon getroffen sind: die Kerzenleuchter stehen schon da, die Kübel mit Stechpalmen—und irgendwo links unter den Füssen des Toten sieht man eine Erhebung, wo das schwarze Tuch sich auf eine befremdende Weise bauscht: dort hat der Mann vom Beerdigungsinstitut den Hammer schon bereit gelegt, mit dem er morgen den Deckel auf den Sarg nageln wird, und man hört jetzt schon, was man morgen erst hören wird: das endgültige nackte Gehämmer, das keine Melodie hat.

HEINRICH BÖLL (1917–   )

aus *Das Brot der frühen Jahre*

in the Wickweber factory, and in each of these holes I saw the front door a hundred times, always the same front door, minute but perfectly formed front doors, finely interlocked like stamps on a large sheet of paper; it was a hundred times over the vision of the man who invented the sparking-plug.

Desperately I looked in my pockets for cigarettes although I knew that I had none left; no doubt there was another packet lying in the car, but the car stood twenty metres to the right from the front door and something like an ocean lay between me and the car. And I thought again of the woman in Kurbel Street, who had wept over the telephone as only women who cannot cope with machines will weep, and all of a sudden I knew that there was no more point in neglecting to think about Ulla, and I thought of her: I did it, just as you suddenly decide to flash on a light in a room where someone has died; in the gloom he had still looked like a sleeper and it was possible to imagine you could still hear his breathing and see him moving; but now a glaring light falls on the scene and you see that the preparations for the funeral rites have already been made: the candlesticks are already standing there, and the tub of holly— and somewhere on the left under the corpse's feet is a lump where the black cloth bulges out in a strange manner: that is where the man from the undertakers' has already laid the hammer which he will use the next day to nail the lid on the coffin, and you can already hear what will only be heard then: the final bleak hammering which plays no tune.

Vocabularies

TRAVELLING BY BOAT	REISEN MIT DEM SCHIFF
basin	{ die Waschschüssel (n) das Waschbecken (–)
berth (sleeping)	die Schlafkoje (n)
captain	der Kapitän (e)
channel	der Ärmelkanal
chimney	der Schornstein (e)
deck	das Deck (s)
destination (country)	der Bestimmungsort (··e)
destination (port)	der Bestimmungshafen (··)
dining-room	der Speisesaal (-säle)
foggy	neblig
foghorn	das Nebelhorn (··er)
life-jacket	die Schwimmweste (n)
lounge	der Aufenthaltsraum (··e)
ocean liner	der Überseedampfer (–)
purser	der Zahlmeister (–)
seasick	seekrank
washroom	der Waschraum (··e)
to berth	{ am Kai festmachen (*reg.*) anlegen (*reg.*)
to disembark	ausschiffen (*reg.*)
to embark	sich einschiffen (*reg.*)

TRAVELLING BY CAR	REISEN MIT DEM AUTO
bend in the road	die Kurve (n)
breakdown	die Panne (n)
breathalyser (to take the – test)	ins Röhrchen pusten
car	{ das Auto (s)
	{ der Wagen (–)
car key	der Autoschlüssel (–)
car park	der Parkplatz ("e)
caravan	der Wohnwagen (–)
chauffeur, paid driver	der Chauffeur (e)
crossing (pedestrian)	der Fussgängerübergang ("e)
dashboard	das Schaltbrett (er)
diversion	die Umleitung (en)
driver	der Fahrer (–)
driving licence	der Führerschein (e)
engine	der Motor (en)
insurance policy	die Versicherungspolice (n)
mechanic	der Mechaniker (–)
motorway	die Autobahn (en)
motel	das Motel (s) —
oil	das Öl
one way street	die Einbahnstrasse (n)
passenger	der Fahrgast ("e)
petrol	das Benzin
petrol station	die Tankstelle (n)
puncture	die Reifenpanne (n)
safety belt	der Sicherheitsgurt (e)
speed limit	die erlaubte Höchstgeschwindkeit
traffic light	die Ampel (n)
tyre	der Reifen (–)
windscreen wiper	der Scheibenwischer (–)
to arrive	ankommen (*irreg.*)
to drive away	wegfahren (*irreg.*)
to tow away	abschleppen (*irreg.*)

TRAVELLING BY PLANE	REISEN MIT DEM FLUGZEUG
aeroplane	das Flugzeug (e)
air-conditioned	klima geregelt
airport	der Flughafen (¨)
airsick	luftkrank
ashtray	der Aschenbecher (–)
cabin	die Kabine (n)
customs	der Zoll
customs official	der Zollbeamte (n)
check-in	die Abfertigung
check-in desk	der Abfertigungschalter (–)
dutiable	verzollbar
duty-free	zollfrei
duty-free goods	das Freigut
hand baggage	das Handgepäck
jet plane	die Düsenmaschine (n)
landing	das Landen
luggage (piece of)	das Gepäckstück (e)
luggage reclaim	die Gepäckablöse (n), die Gepäckausgabe (n)
life-jacket	die Rettungsweste (n)
passport	der Pass (¨e)
pilot	der Pilot (en)
pressurized cabin	die Druckkammer (n)
punctual, on time	rechtzeitig
runway	die Rollbahn (en)
seat-belt	der Sicherheitsgurt (e)
Fasten your seat-belts!	Bitte anschnallen!
steward	der Steward (s)
stewardess	die Stewardesse (n)
take-off	der Abflug (¨e)
ticket	der Flugschein (e)
to check in	abfertigen (reg.)
to declare	verzollen (reg.)
to land	{ landen (reg.) / ankommen (irreg.)
to take off	abfliegen (irreg.)

TRAVELLING BY TRAIN	**REISEN MIT DEM ZUG**
compartment	**das Abteil (e)**
smoking–	**das Raucherabteil (e)**
no smoking–	**das Nichtraucherabteil (e)**
corridor	**der Gang ("e)**
dining car	**der Speisewagen (–)**
engine	**die Lokomotive (n)**
engine driver	**der Lokomotivführer (–)**
fast train	**der Expresszug ("e)**
guard	**der Schaffner (–)**
left luggage office	**die Gepäckaufbewahrung (en)**
lost property office	**das Fundbüro (s)**
luggage van	**der Gepäckwagen (–)**
luggage insurance	**die Gepäckversicherung (en)**
luggage rack	**das Gepäcknetz (e)**
platform	**der Bahnsteig (e)**
porter	**der Gepäckträger (–)**
queue	**die Schlange (n)**
reservation (seat)	**die Platzkarte (n)**
seat	**der Platz ("e)**
sleeping car	**der Schlafwagen (–)**
slow train	**der Bummelzug ("e)**
station	**der Bahnhof ("e)**
supplementary charge	**der Zuschlag ("e)**
ticket (single)	**die Fahrkarte (n)**
„ (return)	**die Rückfahrkarte (n)**
ticket office	**der Fahrkartenschalter (–)**
ticket collector	**der Fahrkartenkontrolleur (e)**
timetable	**der Fahrplan ("e)**
toilet	**die Toilette (n)**
track	**das Geleise (n)**
train	**der Zug ("e)**
Trans European Express	**der TEE**
waiting room	**der Wartesaal (-säle)**
to board	**einsteigen** (*irreg.*)
to get off	**aussteigen** (*irreg.*)
to queue	**Schlange stehen** (*irreg.*)

SHOPS AND SERVICES	GESCHÄFTE UND DIENSTLEISTUNGEN
antique dealer	der Antiquitätenhändler (–)
antique shop	der Antiquitätenladen (··)
art gallery	die Bildergalerie (n)
baker	der Bäcker (–)
bakery	die Bäckerei (en)
bookshop	die Buchhandlung (en)
builder	der Bauunternehmer (–)
butcher	der Metzger (–)
butcher's shop	die Metzgerei (en)
café	das Café (s)
cake shop	die Konditorei (en)
chemist	der Apotheker (–)
chemist's shop	die Apotheke (n)
cinema	das Kino (s)
cleaner's	die Chemische Reinigung
comedy	die Kömodie (n) [(en)
dairy	die Molkerei (en)
decorator	der Tapezierer (–)
dentist	der Zahnarzt (··e)
department store	das Warenhaus (··er)
doctor	der Arzt (··e)
draper	der Tuchwarenhändler (–)
dress shop (ladies')	das Damenkleidergeschäft (e)
dustman	der Müllkastenleerer (–)
electrician	der Elektriker (–)
estate agent	der Makler (–)
film	der Film (e)
fireman	der Feuerwehrmann (··er)
fishmonger	der Fischhändler (–)
garage (repairs)	die Reparaturwerkstätte
gas company	die Gas-Kompanie [(n)
greengrocer's shop	die Obst-und Gemüsehandlung (en)
grocer	der Kolonialwarenhändler (–)
grocery	das Kolonialwarengeschäft (e)

162

hairdresser	der Friseur, der Frisör (e)
hired car	der Mietwagen (–)
hospital	das Krankenhaus (¨er)
ironmonger	das Metallwarengeschäft
jeweller	der Juwelier (e) [(e)
jeweller's shop	das Juwelengeschäft (e)
library	die Bibliothek (en)
market	der Markt (¨e)
museum	das Museum (-seen)
newsagent	der Zeitungshändler (–)
office	das Büro (s)
perfumery	die Parfümerie (n)
play	das Theaterstück (e)
plumber	der Klempner (–)
police station	die Polizei
policeman	{ der Polizist (en), der Schutzmann (¨er)
post office	die Post (en), das Postamt (¨er)
restaurant	das Restaurant (s)
retailer	{ der Kleinhändler (–) der Einzelhändler (–)
shoemaker, cobbler	der Schuhmacher (–)
shoe repair shop	die Schuhmacherei (en)
shoe shop	das Schuhgeschäft (e)
snack bar	die Imbißstube (n)
stationer's	das Papierwarengeschäft (e)
supermarket	der Supermarkt (¨e)
swimming pool	das Schwimmbad (¨er)
tailor	der Schneider (–)
tailor's shop	die Schneiderei (en)
theatre	das Theater (–)
tobacconist	der Tabakhändler (–)
tobacconist's	der Tabakwarenladen (¨)
travel agency	das Reisebüro (s)
wholesaler	der Grosshändler (–)
window cleaner	der Fensterputzer (–)
wine merchant	der Weinhändler (–)
zoo	{ der zoologische Garten (¨) der Zoo (s)
to shop	einkaufen (reg.)

CLOTHING

DIE KLEIDUNG

anorak	der Anorak (e)
apron	die Schürze (n)
bathing costume	der Badeanzug (¨e)
belt	der Gürtel (–)
beret	die Baskenmütze (n)
bikini	der Bikini (s)
blouse	die Bluse (n)
boot	der Stiefel (–)
bow tie	{ die Schleife (n) der Querbinder (–)
braces	die Hosenträger (–)
bra	der Büstenhalter (–)
bracelet	das Armband (¨er)
brooch	die Brosche (n)
buckle	die Schnalle (n)
button	der Knopf (¨e)
buttonhole	das Knopfloch (¨er)
cap	die Kappe (n)
coat	der Mantel (¨)
cape	das Cape (s), der Umhang (¨e)
collar	der Kragen (–)
collar stud	der Kragenknopf (¨e)
corset	das Korsett (s)
cotton	die Baumwolle
cuff	die Manschette (n)
cufflink	der Manschettenknopf (¨e)
curler	der Lockenwickler (–)
dress	das Kleid (er)
dress suit, dinner jacket	der Smoking (s)
dressing gown	der Schlafrock (¨e)
earring	der Ohrring (e)
embroidery	die Stickerei (en)
engagement ring	der Verlobungsring (e)
eyebrow pencil	der Augenbrauenstift (e)
face powder	der Gesichtspuder (–)
fringe	die Franse (n)
glove	der Handschuh (e)
hairslide	die Haarspange (n)

164

hairnet	**das Haarnetz (e)**
hairpin	**die Haarnadel (n)**
hat	**der Hut (··e)**
handkerchief	**das Taschentuch (··er)**
jacket	**die Jacke (n)**
jeans	**die Jeans**
knickers	**die Unterhose (n)**
lace	**die Spitze (n)**
lapel	**das Rever (s)**
lawn (*material*)	**der Batist**
leather	**das Leder**
lipstick	**der Lippenstift (e)**
make-up	**die Schminke**
nail polish	**der Nagellack**
necklace	**die Kette (n)**
nightdress	**das Nachthemd (en)**
nylon	**das Nylon**
overall	**die Kittelschürze (n)**
petticoat	**der Unterrock (··e)**
pocket	**die Tasche (n)**
ponytail	**der Pferdeschwanz (··e)**
powder compact	**die Puderdose (n)**
pyjamas	⎰ **der Schlafanzug (··e)** ⎱ **der Pyjama (s)**
raincoat	**der Regenmantel (··)**
ribbon	**das Band (··er)**
ring	**der Ring (e)**
sandal	**die Sandale (n)**
satin	**der Satin**
scarf	**das Halstuch (··er)**
headscarf	**das Kopftuch (··er)**
shawl	**der Schal (s)**
shirt	**das Oberhemd (en)**
shoe	**der Schuh (e)**
shoelace	**der Schnürsenkel (–)**
silk	**die Seide**
size	**die Grösse (n)**
skirt	**der Rock (··e)**
sleeve	**der Ärmel (–)**
slipper	**der Pantoffel (n)**
sock	**der Socke (n)**
starch	**die Stärke**

stocking	**der Strumpf** (¨e)
suit (man's)	**der Anzug** (¨e)
suit (woman's)	**das Kostüm** (e)
sunglasses	**die Sonnenbrille** (n)
tennis shoe	**der Tennisschuh** (e)
tie	{ **die Kravatte** (n) { **der Schlips** (e)
tights	**die Strumpfhosen**
trousers	**die Hose** (n)
underpants	**die Herrenunterhose** (n)
uniform	**die Uniform** (en)
veil	**der Schleier** (–)
velvet	**der Samt**
waistcoat	**die Weste** (n)
wedding ring	**der Trauring** (e)
wellington boot	**der Gummistiefel** (–)
wig	**die Perücke** (n)
zip	**der Reissverschluss** (¨e)
to change clothes	**sich umziehen** (*irreg.*)
to darn	**stopfen** (*reg.*)
to dress	**sich anziehen** (*irreg.*)
to dryclean	**reinigen** (*reg.*)
to embroider	**sticken** (*reg.*)
to sew	**nähen** (*reg.*)
to try on	**anprobieren** (*reg.*)
to undress	**sich ausziehen** (*irreg.*)

PARTS OF THE BODY — DIE KÖRPERTEILE

ankle	der Knöchel (–)
arm	der Arm (e)
back	der Rücken (–)
backside, bottom	der Hintern (–)
body	der Körper (–)
breast, chest	die Brust (¨e)
cheek	die Backe (n)
chin	das Kinn (e)
ear	das Ohr (en)
eardrum	das Trommelfell (e)
elbow	der Ellbogen (–)
eye	das Auge (n)
eyebrow	die Augenbraue (n)
eyelash	die Augenwimper (n)
finger	der Finger (–)
foot	der Fuss (¨e)
hair	das Haar (e)
hand	die Hand (¨e)
head	der Kopf (¨e)
hip	die Hüfte (n)
jaw	der Kiefer (–)
knee	das Knie (e)
leg	das Bein (e)
lip	die Lippe (n)
mouth	der Mund (¨er)
nail	der Fingernagel (¨)
neck, throat	der Hals (¨e)
nose	die Nase (n)
shoulder	die Schulter (n)
spine	die Wirbelsäule (n)
stomach	der Magen (¨)
thigh	der Oberschenkel (–)
toe	die Zehe (n)
tongue	die Zunge (n)
tooth	der Zahn (¨e)
tummy	der Bauch (¨e)
wrist	das Handgelenk (e)

ESSEN UND TRINKEN

almond	**die Mandel (n)**
anchovy	**die Sardelle (n)**
apple	**der Apfel (¨)**
apricot	**die Aprikose (n)**
artichoke	**die Artischoke (n)**
asparagus	**der Spargel (n)**
aubergine	**die Aubergine (n)**
avocado	**die Avocado (s)**
bacon	**der Speck**
banana	**die Banane (n)**
bean (French)	**die grüne Bohne (n)**
beef	**das Rindfleisch**
beer	**das Bier (e)**
beetroot	**die rote Rübe (n)**
bilberry	**die Heidelbeere (n)**
biscuit	**der Keks (e)**
blackberry	**die Brombeere (n)**
blackcurrant	**die schwarze Johannisbeere (n)**
bloater	**der Bückling (e)**
boiled	**gekocht**
bone	**der Knochen (–)**
brain	**das Gehirn (e)**
brandy	**der Cognak**
brazil nut	**die Paranuss (¨e)**
bread	**das Brot (e)**
black	**das Schwarzbrot (e)**
white	**das Weissbrot (e)**
black rye	**das Pumpernickel**
rye	**das Roggenbrot (e)**
roll	**das Brötchen (–)**
crusty roll	**die Brezel (n)**
poppy-seed roll	**das Mohnbrötchen (–)**
breadcrumb	**der Brotsamen (–)**
broth	**die Kraftbrühe (n)**
Brussels sprouts	**der Rosenkohl**
butter	**die Butter**
cabbage	**der Kohl**
pickled	**das Sauerkraut**
red	**das Rotkraut**

savoy	**der Wirsingkohl**
cake	**der Kuchen (–)**
cheese	**der Käsekuchen (–)**
sponge	**der Rührkuchen (–)**
caper	**die Kaper (n)**
caraway seed	**der Kümmel**
cheese	**der Käse (–)**
cherry	**die Kirsche (n)**
chicken	**das Huhn (¨er)**
„ (small)	**das Hähnchen (–)**
chive	**der Schnittlauch**
chocolate	**die Schokolade (n)**
chocolate bar	**die Tafel Schokolade (Tafeln)**
chocolate cream	**die Praline (n)**
chop	**das Kotelett (s)**
cider	**der Apfelwein (e)**
cocoa	**der Kakao**
coconut	**die Kokosnuss (¨e)**
cod	**der Kabeljau (s)**
coffee	**der Kaffee (s)**
iced	**der Eiskaffee (s)**
cornflour	**das Maismehl**
crab	**der Krebs (e)**
cream	**die Sahne**
whipped	**die Schlagsahne**
cucumber	**die Gurke (n)**
pickled	**die Salzgurke (n)**
date	**die Dattel (n)**
dessert	**der Nachtisch (e)**
diet	**die Diät (en)**
dough	**der Teig (e)**
duck	**die Ente (n)**
egg	**das Ei (er)**
fried	**das Spiegelei (er)**
scrambled	**das Rührei (er)**
escallop	**das Schnitzel (n)**
fat, lard	**das Fett**
fish	**der Fisch (e)**
fried	**der Backfisch (e)**
fizzy	**sprudelnd**
flour	**das Mehl**

fruit	{ das Obst (-arten)
	die Frucht ("e)
fruit flan	der Obstkuchen (–)
game	das Wild
garlic	der Knoblauch (e)
gateau	die Torte (n)
gherkin	die Essiggurke (n)
sweet-sour gherkin	die süßsaure Gurke (n)
giblets	die Hühnerinnereien
gin	der Gin
goose	die Gans ("e)
gooseberry	die Stachelbeere (n)
grape	die Traube (n)
grapefruit	die Pampelmuse (n)
green pepper	der Schotenpfeffer (–)
greengage	die Reineclaude (n)
haddock	der Schellfisch (e)
hake	der Seehecht (e)
halibut	der Heilbutt (e)
ham	der Schinken
cured	der Rohschinken
hare	der Hase (–)
hazelnut	die Haselnuss ("e)
heart	das Herz (en)
herb	das Küchenkraut ("er)
herring	der Hering (e)
smoked	der geräucherte Hering (e)
pickled	der Rollmops ("e)
ice cream	das Eis, das Gefrorene
ice cube	das Eis, das Eisstück (e)
icing sugar	der Puderzucker
jam, marmalade	die Marmelade (n)
jelly	der Gelee (s)
kidney	die Niere (n)
lamb	das Lamm
lemon	die Zitrone (n)
lemon juice	der Zitronensaft ("e)
lemonade	das Zitronat
lentil	die Linse (n)
lettuce	der Kopfsalat (e)
liver	die Leber
calf's	die Kalbsleber

chicken	die Hühnerleber
paté	die Leberpastete (n)
lobster	{ der Hummer (–)
	die Languste (n)
lollipop	das Lutschbonbon (s)
macaroon	die Makrone (n)
mackerel	die Makrele (n)
marrow	das Mark (die Markgemüse)
marzipan	das Marzipan
meat	das Fleisch
melon	die Melone (n)
meringue	die Meringe (n)
milk	die Milch
mince, minced meat	das Hackfleisch
mineral water	das Mineralwasser
mustard	der Senf
nougat	das Nougat
nutmeg	die Muskatnuss (¨e)
oil	das Öl
olive	die Olive (n)
omelette	das Omelett (s)
onion	die Zwiebel (n)
orange	{ die Orange (n)
	die Apfelsine (n)
orange juice	der Orangensaft (¨e)
orangeade	die Orangeade
oyster	die Auster (n)
pancake	der Pfannkuchen (–)
paprika	das Paprika
parsley	die Petersilie
pastry (puff)	der Blätterteig (e)
„ (short)	der Mürbeteig (e)
peach	der Pfirsich (e)
peanut	die Erdnuss (¨e)
pear	die Birne (n)
pepper	der Pfeffer
pheasant	der Fasan (en)
picnic	das Picknick (e)
pigeon	die Taube (n)
pineapple	die Ananas (–, or e)
plaice	die Scholle (n)

plum	die Pflaume (n)
poached	pochiert
egg	das verlorene Ei
pork	das Schweinefleisch
port	der Port
potato	die Kartoffel (n)
fried	die Bratkartoffel (n)
in jacket	die Pellkartoffel (n)
poultry	das Geflügel
prawn	die Garnele (n)
prune	die Backpflaume (n)
quail	die Wachtel (n)
rabbit	das Kaninchen (–)
radish	der Rettich (e)
small red	das Radischen (–)
raisin	die Rosine (n)
raspberry	die Himbeere (n)
redcurrant	die Johannisbeere (n)
rhubarb	der Rhabarber
rice	der Reis
boiled	gekochter Reis
rice pudding	der Reispudding (s or e)
roast	der Braten (–)
roe (hard)	der Fischlaich
„ (soft)	der Milchner
rum	der Rum
salmon	der Lachs
smoked	der geräucherte Lachs (e)
salt	das Salz
sandwich	das belegte Brot (e)
„ (roll)	das belegte Brötchen (–)
sardine	die Sardine (n)
sauce	die Sosse, die Sauce (n)
salami	die Salami
sausage	die Wurst ("e)
Bologna	die Mettwurst ("e)
Frankfurters	die Frankfurter Würstchen
ham	die Schinkenwurst ("e)
liver	die Leberwurst ("e)
scallop	die Kammuschel (n)
seasoning	das Gewürz (e)
semolina	der Griess

172

shallot	die Schalotte (n)
smoked	geräuchert
shortbread	der Mürbeteig (e)
sherry	der Sherry
soda water	das Sodawasser, das Sprudel
sole	die Seezunge (n)
soup	die Suppe (n)
clear	die Brühe (n)
thick	die dicke Suppe (n)
spaghetti	die Spaghetti (s)
spinach	der Spinat
starter	die Vorspeise, (n), das Hors d'oeuvre
steak	das Steak (s)
stew	das Schmorgericht (e)
still (drink)	schäumend
strawberry	die Erdbeere (n)
stuffed	gefüllt
stuffing	die Füllung (en)
sugar	der Zucker
sultana	die Sultanine (n)
sweet	das Bonbon (s)
syrup	der Sirup
tangerine	die Mandarine (n)
tea	der Tee
toast	der Toast
toffee	das Sahnebonbon (s)
tomato	die Tomate (n)
tripe	die Kutteln
trout	die Forelle (n)
turbot	der Steinbutt (e)
turkey	der Truthahn (¨e), die Pute (n)
turnip	die Rübe (n)
vanilla	die Vanille
veal	das Kalbfleisch
vegetable	das Gemüse (–)
venison	der Rehrücken (–)
vinegar	der Essig
vitamin	das Vitamin (e)
walnut	die Walnuss (¨e)

water	**das Wasser**
watercress	**die Brunnenkresse**
whiting	**der Weissfisch** (e)
wine	**der Wein** (e)
sweet	**der Süsswein** (e)
red	**der Rotwein** (e)
white	**der Weisswein** (e)
winkle	**die Strandschnecke** (n)
woodcock	**die Waldschnepfe** (n)
yoghurt	**der Joghurt**

GERMAN
IN THREE MONTHS

III

KEY TO GRAMMAR EXERCISES
AND INDEX TO GRAMMAR

KEY TO LESSON 1

Exercise I

1 I am not. 2 You are. 3 Is he? 4 It is not. 5 Are you not?
6 Sie sind nicht. 7 Sind wir? 8 Sie sind nicht. 9 Ist sie?
10 Ich bin.

Exercise II

1 We were. 2 They were not. 3 Was he not? 4 I was not.
5 Was she? 6 Sie waren nicht. 7 Waren Sie? 8 Er war nicht.
9 Waren sie nicht? 10 Waren Sie nicht?

Exercise III

1 Who is here? 2 Where were you? 3 I was here. 4 Are
they here to-day? 5 No, they were here yesterday. 6 Is he at
home to-day? 7 No, he was at home yesterday. 8 How is
that? 9 This is nice. 10 Where am I? 11 Ist es klein?
12 Nein, es ist nicht klein. 13 Wo waren Sie gestern? 14 Ich
war zu Hause. 15 Ist er oben? 16 Nein, er ist nicht unten,
er ist oben. 17 Wir waren zu Hause. 18 Sind sie hier?
19 Ja, sie sind oben. 20 Was ist er? 21 Wie war das?

KEY TO LESSON 2

Exercise I

1 What are you doing to-day? 2 We played yesterday.
3 How much is that? 4 It costs nothing. 5 He sold everything. 6 I made it so. 7 Ich wohne hier. 8 Wo wohnen Sie?
9 Was rauchte er? 10 Ich höre nichts. 11 Was holen sie?

Exercise II

1 What are you learning? 2 We were learning German.
3 Has she much money? 4 No, she has not much money.
5 What did he have? 6 He had nothing. 7 Kauften Sie
etwas? 8 Nein, ich kaufte nichts. 9 Wer spielte? 10 Wir
spielten gestern. 11 War er gestern hier? 12 Ja, er war
gestern hier.

Exercise III

1 Er spricht Deutsch gut. 2 Sie liest ein Buch. 3 Er nimmt
die Briefe. 4 Sie vergisst oft alles. 5 Schläft er lange?

KEY TO LESSON 4

Exercise I

1 Wo ist der Wagen? 2 Er ist hier. 3 Haben Sie einen Kugelschreiber? 4 Ja, ich habe einen. 5 Wo ist die Uhr? 6 Sie ist hier. 7 Haben Sie die Postkarte? 8 Ja, ich habe sie. 9 Bitte bestellen Sie ein Taxi. 10 Es kommt sofort. 11 Ich möchte eine Zeitung. 12 Wieviel kostet sie? 13 Wieviel kostet der Bleistift? 14 Er kostet dreissig Pfennig.

Exercise II

1 Sehen Sie ihn? 2 Nein, ich sehe ihn nicht. 3 Ich kaufe einen Bleistift. 4 Is das Ihr Büro? 5 Ja, es ist mein Büro. 6 Hier ist unser Tisch. 7 Wo ist er? 8 Kennen Sie seine Sekretärin? 9 Nein, ich kenne sie nicht. 10 Wann möchten Sie den Wagen? 11 Ich möchte ihn sofort.

Exercise III

1 Wohin setzen Sie sich? 2 Ich sitze hier. 3 Wie fühlen Sie sich? 4 Ich fühle mich wohl. 5 Wäscht er sich? 6 Ja, er wäscht sich. 7 Freut er sich? 8 Ja, er freut sich. 9 Freut sie sich auf die Ferien? 10 Ja, sie freut sich darauf. (See Lesson 11) 11 Bezahlten Sie die Rechnung? 12 Nein, ich bezahlte sie nicht. 13 Sie unterhalten sich lange.

KEY TO LESSON 5

Exercise I

1. Haben Sie einen Teppich gekauft? 2 Nein, ich habe keinen Teppich gekauft. 3 Hat er einen Tisch bestellt? 4 Ja, der Tisch ist bestellt. 5 Haben sie den Ring verkauft? 6 Ja, sie haben den Ring verkauft. 7 Der Lehrer hat die Frage wiederholt.

Exercise II

1 Im Frühling blühen die Blumen. 2 Hat sie genug Geld die Rechnung zu bezahlen? 3 Mein Freund hat gestern telephoniert. 4 Am Sonntag haben wir das Hotel besucht. 5 Wo haben Sie gelebt? 6 In England? 7 Ja, ich habe in England gelebt.

A short story

Mr. Schulz comes home early to-day. He did not have much work to-day. His wife and the children have already been waiting for him. They are all hungry. She has already prepared the dinner. To-day the dinner consists of soup, a roast and vegetable. To finish with, she served a bowl of fruit. The family spends the evening at home. Mr. Schulz reads a newspaper and his wife knits a pullover. The children do their home work and then sit themselves before the television to watch a film. Mr. Schulz does not watch the television, he works some more and then they all go to bed. They are very tired.

KEY TO LESSON 6

Exercise I

1 Können Sie das lesen? 2 Ja, ich kann. 3 Will er nach Hause gehen? 4 Nein, er will hier bleiben. 5 Müssen Sie die Wohnung verkaufen? 6 Ja, leider muss ich sie verkaufen. 7 Wir möchten gern eine Tasse Kaffee. 8 Will sie am Sonntag kommen? 9 Nein, sie will am Samstag kommen.

Exercise II

1 Darf er das Fenster öffnen? 2 Natürlich darf er. 3 Sie muss das Essen vorbereiten. 4 Es muss um sieben Uhr fertig sein. 5 Können Sie diesen Geldschein wechseln? 6 Nein, ich kann es nicht, ich habe kein Kleingeld.

Exercise III

1 Kannst du mich morgen besuchen? 2 Ja, ich kann kommen. 3 Kauf das Haus! 4 Lernt Deutsch! 5 Fragen Sie ihn! 6 Schlafen Sie gut!

KEY TO LESSON 7

Exercise I

1 Die Dame reist mit ihrem Mann nach Deutschland. 2 Wir wohnen nicht bei ihm. 3 Der Beamte gibt dem Ausländer einen Zettel. 4 Er gibt mir seine Adresse. 5 Holen Sie ihm die Zeitung. 6 Zeigen Sie mir Ihren Pass.

Exercise II

1 Sehen Sie ihn? 2 Ja, ich kann ihn sehen. 3 Was kaufen Sie sich? 4 Ich kaufe mir einen Mantel. 5 Zeigen Sie ihr die Bilder? 6 Ja, ich will sie ihr zeigen. 7 Hilft er Ihnen bei der Arbeit? 8 Nein, er hilft mir nicht. 9 Tut es Ihnen leid? 10 Ja, es tut mir sehr leid.

KEY TO LESSON 8

Exercise I

1 Sahen Sie den Unfall? 2 Nein, ich sah ihn nicht. 3 Schrieb sie ihrem Freund einen Brief? 3 Ja, sie schrieb ihm. 5 Gingen Sie gestern abend ins Kino? 6 Nein, wir gingen nicht. 7 Konnte er den Wagen reparieren? 8 Ja, der Wagen ist repariert. 9 Riefen Sie Ihre Freundin an? 10 Ja, aber sie war nicht zu Hause.

A short story

Mr. Maier had an accident yesterday. A driver collided with him in a one way street. The driver had entered the one way street from the wrong end. At first Mr. Maier was very angry. He wanted to make a few more purchases quickly and then meet his wife in town. Both drivers exchanged addresses. They wanted to get in touch with each other again. Mr. Maier went to his garage and asked Mr. Schulz to repair the car. He promised to have the car repaired as soon as possible. Mr. Maier called a taxi and went to the café to meet his wife.

Exercise II

1 Konnten Sie sie besuchen? 2 Ja, ich besuchte sie letzte Woche. 3 Musste er zurückgehen? 4 Nein, er konnte hier bleiben. 5 Durfte das Kind ausgehen? 6 Ja, die Eltern erlaubten es. 7 Wollte sie mit dem Wagen fahren? 8 Nein, sie wollte mit dem Flugzeug fliegen. 9 Gewann die Mannschaft das Fussballspiel? Ja, das Resultat war 2:1 (zwei zu eins).

KEY TO LESSON 9

Exercise I

1 Sie hat einen Pelzmantel gekauft. 2 Ich habe früher in London gewohnt. 3 Sie haben uns ihren Laden gezeigt. 4 Haben Sie ihn gefragt? 5 Unsere Ferien haben viel Geld gekostet.

Exercise II

1 Haben Sie die Garage gemietet? 2 Nein, ich habe sie nicht mieten können. 3 Hat er zu viel getrunken? 4 Nein, er ist ganz nüchtern. 5 Haben Sie mein Buch gelesen? 6 Ja, ich habe es sehr interessant gefunden. 7 Haben Sie ihn bewundern müssen? 8 Ja. ich habe ihn immer bewundert. 9 Hat er dorthin gehen wollen? 10 Nein, er hat nicht dorthin gehen wollen.

Exercise III

1 Hat sie die Strasse überquert? 2 Nein, sie ist auf dem Bürgersteig geblieben. 3 Ist sie ins Büro geeilt? 4 Ja, der Zug hatte Verspätung. 5 Ist das Gras wieder gewachsen? 6 Nein, es ist noch immer sehr gelb.

KEY TO LESSON 10

Exercise I

1 Konnten Sie meinen Freunden das Geld leihen? 2 Ja, ich konnte es ihnen leihen. 3 Waren diese Häuser sehr teuer? 4 Nien, sie sind sehr preiswert. 5 Sind die Hotels alle voll? 6 Nein, einige haben noch Zimmer frei. 7 Dürfen wir die Äpfel von diesen Bäumen pflücken? 8 Warum nicht, da sind viele. 9 Sind die Gäste ins Kino gegangen? 10 Leider waren keine Plätze mehr frei.

Exercise II

1 Hat der Mann seine Frau besucht? 2 Ja, aber sie war weg. 3 Ist der Käse in England erhältlich? 4 Nein, man kann ihn dort nicht bekommen. 5 War dieses Restaurant geschlossen? 6 Nein, es ist jeden Tag von 10 Uhr morgens bis Mitternacht geöffnet. 7 Welches Hotel können Sie empfehlen? 8 Ich kann keins empfehlen. 9 Welcher Kellner bringt unsere Bestellung? 10 Dieser Kellner kommt gerade.

Exercise III

1 Wohin gehen Sie? 2 Ich gehe auf die Post (or) zum Postamt. 3 Was wollen Sie am Schalter kaufen? 4 Ich will Briefmarken kaufen. 5 Wohin können Sie den Kalender hängen? 6 Ich kann ihn an die Wand hängen. 7 Hat Ihr Bruder Ihnen das Geschenk gegeben? 8 Nein, meine Schwester gab es mir. 9 Hat ihr dieses Gericht geschmeckt? 10 Ja, es schmeckte ihr sehr gut.

KEY TO LESSON 11

Exercise I

1 Ist Ihr Grossvater gestern abend gestorben? 2 Ja, er starb auf eine friedliche Art. 3 Hat der Mann eine blinde Frau? 4 Nein, er hat eine taube Frau. 5 Ist Ihr kluger Freund sehr einsam? 6 Nein, er hat viele intelligente Freunde.

Exercise II

1 Womit bezahlten Sie die hohe Rechnung? 2 Ich bezahlte mit einem Scheck. 3 Woraus trank er den neuen Wein? 4 Er trank aus einem alten Glas. 5 Woraus haben Sie den Anzug genommen? 6 Ich habe ihn aus dem Koffer genommen.

Exercise III

1 Was für eine Strasse ist das? 2 Das ist eine ruhige Strasse. 3 Was für ein Büro ist das? 4 Das ist ein kleines Büro. 5 Was für eine Familie ist das? 6 Das ist eine nette Familie.

KEY TO LESSON 12

Exercise I

1 Trinken Sie lieber Tee oder Kaffee? 2 Ich trinke lieber Kaffee. 3 War das Wetter kälter im Januar oder Februar letztes Jahr? 4 Es war im Februar kälter. 5 War der Soldat berühmter als der Matrose? 6 Der Matrose war der berühmteste.

Exercise II

1 Sind diese Zeitungen interessant? 2 Nein, die Bücher sind viel interessanter. 3 Ist das Ihr neuester Koffer? 4 Nein, das

ist mein ältester Koffer. 5 Können Sie mir den kürzesten Weg zur Bank zeigen? 6 Ja, aber der kürzeste Weg ist nicht immer der beste.

Exercise III

1 Hat er versprochen fleissiger zu arbeiten? 2 Ja, er hat es versprochen. 3 Hörten Sie ihn die Treppe heraufkommen? 4 Nein, ich hörte ihn nicht, er war sehr leise. 5 Was gab es dort zu sehen? 6 Dort gab es nicht viel zu sehen.

KEY TO LESSON 13

Exercise I

1 Kennen Sie den Bruder dieser Dame? 2 Nein, ich kenne ihn nicht. 3 Wo ist das Büro Ihrer Firma? 4 Es ist an der Ecke der nächsten Strasse. 5 Ist das der Wagen Ihres Schwagers? 6 Nein, das ist nicht sein Wagen, er ist der Wagen meiner Schwägerin.

Exercise II

1 Kaufen Sie Blumen für Ihre Gastgeberin? 2 Nein, ich kaufe Pralinen, anstatt Blumen. 3 Trafen Sie viele Leute während Ihres Aufenthaltes in Deutschland? 4 Ja, ich traf viele alte Freunde. 5 Wo ist das Rathaus dieser Stadt? 6 Sie werden es auf dem Marktplatz finden.

KEY TO LESSON 14

Exercise I

1 Wo wohnt er? 2 Er wohnt in London. 3 Wie geht es Ihnen? 4 Es geht mir sehr gut, danke. 5 Wieviel kostet dieses Paar Schuhe? 6 Sie kosten hundert zehn DM. (Mark). 7 Wann kommt sie das nächste Mal? 8 Sie wird nächste Woche kommen. 9 Wessen Geburtstag ist heute? 10 Es ist der Geburtstag meines Sohnes.

Exercise II

1 Schreiben Sie an Herrn Schmidt? 2 Ja, ich schreibe an ihn. 3 Werden Sie Ihren Kollegen einladen? 4 Nein, ich will ihn nicht einladen. 5 Wo ist der Hund seines Nachbars? 6 Er

ist davongelaufen. 7 Wie ist der Name Ihres Bekannten?
8 Es tut mir leid, aber ich kenne seinen Namen nicht.

Exercise III

1 Ist die Stellung des Angestellten gut bezahlt? 2 Ja, sie ist
sehr gut bezahlt. 3 Ist der Wartesaal nur für Reisende?
4 Nein, alle können ihn benutzen. 5 Mit wem haben Sie
gesprochen? 6 Ich habe mit dem Beamten gesprochen.
7 Welches Datum haben wir heute? 8 Heute ist der 20
Dezember 1978 (zwanzigste Dezember neunzehnhundert
achtundsiebzig).

KEY TO LESSON 15

Exercise I

1 Wo kann ich eine Fahrkarte bekommen? 2 Wenn Sie eine
Fahrkarte kaufen wollen, müssen Sie zum Fahrkarten-
schalter gehen. 3 Kommt er nicht, weil es schneit? 4 Oh,
doch, er kommt, obgleich es schneit. 5 Wo wohnen Sie in
London? 6 Als ich das letzte Mal in London war, wohnte ich
bei Freunden.

Exercise II

1 Wissen Sie, wann der Bus ankommt? 2 Nein, ich weiss die
genaue Zeit nicht. 3 Ist Ihr Teilhaber krank gewesen?
4 Nein, aber jedesmal, wenn ich mit ihm sprechen wollte,
war er nicht da. 5 Können Sie mir sagen, wann das Schiff
in Southampton anlegt? 6 Als wir das letzte Mal dort
anlegten, mussten wir lange auf den Zollbeamten warten.

KEY TO LESSON 16

Exercise I

1 Wo ist die Schreibmaschine, auf der (worauf) Sie den Brief
schreiben wollen? 2 Sie steht direkt vor Ihnen. 3 Ist das das
Hotel, in dem (worin) Sie für uns ein Zimmer reserviert
haben? 4 Nein, es ist auf der anderen Seite der Strasse. 5 Ist
das der Zeitungsartikel, wovon Sie gesprochen haben? 6 Ja,
das ist der Artikel, den ich sehr interessant fand. 7 Sind das

die Würste, deren Häute so zäh sind? 8 Nein, das sind nicht die gleichen.

Exercise II

1 Er gab mir einen Kassettenrekorder, der sehr teuer war. 2 Wie gefallen Ihnen die Möbel, die ich im Ausverkauf gekauft habe? 3 Ich machte ein neues Gericht, das allen sehr gut schmeckte. 4 Die neue Aktentasche, worin (in der) er seine Dokumente trägt, war sehr woll. 5 Können Sie mir ein Buch empfehlen, woraus ich lernen kann? 6 Was immer er sagte, war sinnlos.

KEY TO LESSON 17

Exercise I

1 Was für ein Programm hast du (habt ihr) gestern abend im Fernsehen gesehen? 2 Wir haben unser Lieblingsprogramm gesehen. 3 Hattest du (hattet ihr) letzten Sommer schöne Ferien gehabt? 4 Nein, es war viel zu heiss. 5 Erwartest du (erwartet ihr) nächsten Frühling deine (eure) beste Freundin? 6 Ja, ich erwarte sie.

Exercise II

1 Sollen wir dir (euch) einen Scheck für die Transaktion geben? 2 Ja, vielen Dank, ich bin etwas knapp bei Kasse. 3 Was machst du (macht ihr) am nächsten Sonntag? 4 Wir werden zu dir (zu euch) zum Tee kommen. 5 Ich möchte dir (euch) für deine (für eure) Freundlichkeit danken. 6 Nichts zu danken, es ist gern geschehen.

KEY TO LESSON 18

Exercise I

1 Haben Sie den Brief zur Post gebracht? 2 Ja, ich habe ihn eingeworfen. 3 Wie benützt man das Telefon in der Telefonzelle? 4 Sie müssen 20 Pfennig einwerfen. 5 Wann ist er gestern aufgestanden? 6 Er stand gegen Mittag auf.

Exercise II

1 Waren Sie überrascht, als er Ihnen den Brief nachschickte? 2 Nein, ich habe ihn erwartet. 3 Kann sich das Kind schon

185

selbst anziehen? 4 Ja, es kann es selbst tun. 5 Sind Sie schon in der neuen Ausstellung gewesen? 6 Nein, aber ich will sie mir ansehen.

Exercise III

1 Lassen Sie mich Ihrem Brief einen Gruss hinzufügen? 2 Warum nicht, hier ist er. 3 Kann ich eine Tasse Kaffee haben, bitte? 4 Gut, ich werde Ihnen ein Kännchen Kaffee in Ihr Zimmer schicken lassen. 5 Haben Sie den Brief übersetzen lassen? 6 Ja, aber sie fanden ihn sehr schwer.

KEY TO LESSON 19

Exercise I

1 Wird es morgen regnen? 2 Nein, ich glaube nicht. 3 Studiert er in Deutschland? 4 Nein, aber er wird dort studieren. 5 Ist sie reich geworden? 6 Ja, eine alte Tante hat ihr viel Geld hinterlassen.

Exercise II

1 Wurde der Mann bei dem Unfall verletzt? 2 Ja, er ist gerade operiert worden. 3 Wird das Konzert im Radio übertragen? 4 Ja, Sie können es heute abend hören. 5 Wo wird die Zeitung gedruckt? 6 Sie wird in London gedruckt werden.

Exercise III

1 Können Sie um 8 Uhr zum Essen kommen? 2 Wenn es mir rechtzeitig gesagt wird, werde ich um 8 Uhr kommen können. 3 Wann wird das Buch verlegt werden? 4 Wenn der Schriftsteller überredet werden kann, wird es im Sommer erscheinen. 5 Von wem wird er untersucht? 6 Der Arzt, der in Kürze gerufen werden darf, wird ihn untersuchen können.

KEY TO LESSON 20

Exercise I

1 Folgte man Ihnen zum Bahnhof? 2 Nein, ich habe nichts Besonderes bemerkt. 3 Was hat man Ihnen befohlen, in dieser Sache zu tun? 4 Man befahl mir, die Sache der

Polizei zu melden. 5 Hat man ihm das Rauchen verboten?
6 Ja, ich glaube, aber er hat beschlossen weniger zu rauchen.

Exercise II

1 Ist ihr die Ankunft des Flugzeuges mitgeteilt worden? 2 Ja,
man hat es ihr mitgeteilt. 3 Hat man ihm erzählt, dass die
Steuern erhöht worden sind? 4 Nein, er hatte keine Ahnung
davon. 5 War es sehr stürmisch, als Sie über den See fuhren?
6 Nein, der See war ganz windstill. 7 Schliessen die Banken
samstags? 8 Ja, sie sind geschlossen.

KEY TO LESSON 21

Exercise I

1 Können Sie mir sagen, wo man hier die beste Tasse Kaffee
bekommt? 2 Ja, den besten Kaffee bekommen Sie im Schloss
Café. 3 Wie ist das Wetter im Sommer in England? 4 Es
ist am heissesten im Juli und im August. 5 Warum geht er
immer hin und her? 6 Er geht immer hin und her, weil er
nervös ist.

Exercise II

1 Welches ist die billigere Reise, die nach Holland oder die in
die Schweiz? 2 Die Reise nach Holland ist die billigere.
3 Ist dies der höchste Kirchturm in Europa? 4 Ja, er ist der
höchste. 5 Sind Sie die Treppe hinaufgegangen und haben
das Fahrrad heruntergeholt? 6 Nein, ich habe es nicht
heruntergebracht, weil ich es nicht gefunden habe.

Exercise III

1 Hat er sich nach dem Zug erkundigt? 2 Ja, er hat die
nötigen Erkundigungen eingeholt. 3 Haben Sie über seine
Antwort gesprochen? 4 Ja, wir haben darüber gesprochen.
5 Hat sie Sie um Hilfe gebeten? 6 Nein, sie hat mich nicht
darum gebeten. 7 Haben Sie sich vor dem Hund gefürchtet?
8 Nein, ich habe mich nicht vor ihm gefürchtet.

KEY TO LESSON 22

Exercise I

1 Täten Sie das an meiner Stelle? 2 Ja, ich täte das gleiche.
3 Sagte er, dass er den Bericht geschrieben hätte? 4 Nein, das

187

hat er nicht gesagt. 5 Könnten Sie mich wissen lassen, ob der Ausschuss schon einen Entschluss gefasst hat? 6 Ja, der Entschluss ist gestern gefasst worden.

Exercise II

1 Was käme für Sie in Frage? 2 Ich möchte ein Paar Schuhe und eine passende Handtasche. 3 Könnten Sie mir Ihren Feldstecher leihen, so dass ich das Rennen sehen kann? 4 Ja, natürlich, aber bitte geben Sie ihn mir bald zurück. 5 Möchten Sie mit mir ins Kino gehen? 6 Das ist sehr nett von Ihnen, aber ich ginge lieber ins Theater.

Translation into German

Der Chauffeur sagte, er sei (wäre) ganz fertig. Ich fragte ihn, ob er wüsste, um wievel Uhr wir ankämen. Er sagte, er wäre nicht sicher. Unterwegs fragten wir einen Polizisten, ob wir auf dem richtigen Weg wären. Er sagte, er sei nicht sicher, aber er könnte seinen Mitarbeiter fragen. Der Chauffeur meinte, das sei nicht nötig und wir fuhren weiter.

KEY TO LESSON 23

Exercise I

1 Würden Sie einen Wagen von diesem Mann kaufen, wenn er ein Händler wäre? 2 Nein, ich traue ihm nicht und würde keinen Wagen von ihm kaufen. 3 Hätte sie für mich diesen Fernanruf gemacht, wenn ich dafür bezahlt hätte? 4 Ich bin nicht sicher, ob sie die richtige Vorwählnummer kennt. 5 Wenn er mit Ihnen ginge, würden Sie ihn begleiten? 6 Nein, ich würde ihn nicht begleiten, da er nicht mein Typ ist.

Exercise II

1 Wenn ich Ihnen meine Visitenkarte gäbe, könnten Sie mir seine Adresse schicken? 2 Das wäre möglich. 3 Hat Ihr Freund beim Skilaufen einen Knöchel gebrochen? 4 Nein, hätte er seinen Knöchel gebrochen, so hätte er nicht zurückfliegen können. 5 Wüsste Ihre Tochter was sie mit ihrer Erbschaft tun sollte? 6 Nein, sie wüsste bestimmt nicht, wie sie das Geld anlegen sollte.

Translate into German

Würden Sie mit mir in ein gutes Restaurant gehen, wenn ich Sie einladen würde? Ich würde sehr gern mitgehen, wenn Sie mir vorher. Bescheid gäben. Gut, das könnte ich machen. Würde es Ihnen passen, wenn wir uns am nächsten Freitag um 8 Uhr unter der grossen Uhr am Hauptbahnhof träfen? Das wäre sehr nett, solange nichts in der Zwischenzeit passiert. Hätten Sie gern, dass ich die Verabredung bestätige? Das wäre sehr aufmerksam. Vielen Dank im voraus, ich freue mich sehr auf den Abend.

KEY TO LESSON 24

Exercise I

1 Hat er sich über das unerwartete Geschenk gewundert? 2 Nein, aber ich habe mich sehr darüber gefreut. 3 Als Sie krank waren, ist Ihnen schwindlig gewesen? 4 Ja, es wird mir immer noch schwindlig. 5 Fehlt es den Lehrern immer an Geld? 6 Nein, im Augenblick werden sie besser bezahlt.

Exercise II

1 Gibt es ein besonders interresantes Museum in Ihrer Stadt? 2 Ja, es gibt dort viele. 3 Ist ein fertig gebackener Kuchen in der Tiefkühltruhe? 4 Nein, ich habe heute keinen neuen gemacht. 5 Ärgern Sie sich über den unaufhaltsamen Regen? 6 Ja, und die rutschigen Strassen sind sehr gefährlich.

Exercise III

1 Wen kann man um elf Uhr nachts auf dem Heimweg treffen? 2 Man kann die singenden, lärmenden Menschen, die aus der Wirtschaft kommen, treffen. 3 Wer gefällt ihm am besten? 4 Die kichernden und lachenden Mädchen gefallen ihm am besten. 5 Ist das die gleiche Zeitung wie die meinige? (oder wie meine) 6 Nein, es ist nicht die gleiche. 7 Wo ist denn unser Hund geblieben? 8 Ich habe den Ihrigen (Ihren) nirgends gesehen.

Index

Adjectives
after noun   64
comparison of   69, 113
declension of   59, 64–5, 132
forming negative with *un-*   133
possessive   28, 43, 132

Adverbs
of time, manner, place   85
forming negative with *un-*   133
order of   86

Articles
definite and indefinite   22, 25
nominative of   27
accusative of   27
dative of   42
genitive of   74
plural of   59

Conjunctions
not affecting word order   76, 84
subordinate   84
wenn in conditional sentences   124–5

Nouns
gender of   22–25
nominative of   28
accusative of   28
dative of   42, 59
genitive of   74–5
plural of   57–9
weak   80–1
with different meanings   109

Prepositions
governing accusative   44
governing dative   44–5
governing acc. or dative   60
governing genitive   75
prefixed by *wo* and *da*   65, 90

Pronouns
nominative of   28
accusative of   28, 48
dative of   43
familiar forms   38, 93–4
interrogative   79
reflexive   28, 97
relative   89

Verbs
regular
present tense   18, 20
imperfect tense   18, 19
perfect tense   31–3, 54
pluperfect tense   55
future tense   102
conditional tense   124–5
subjunctive   117–8
irregular
present tense   18, 20
imperfect tense   48
perfect tense   31–3, 55
subjunctive   119–20
auxiliary
haben   19, 31, 118
sein   15, 16, 119
present tense   15, 36
imperfect tense   16, 49
perfect tense   53
subjunctive   119
in passive sentences   105
followed by certain prepositions   114–5
governing accusative   61
governing dative   45–6, 61
imperative mood   38
impersonal verbs   46, 130
infinitive sentences   71